THE NEW BOOK OF
BASEBALL
TRIVIA

MORE THAN
500 QUESTIONS
FOR AVID FANS

WAYNE STEWART

SPORTS
PUBLISHING

Sports Publishing books may be purchased in bulk at special discounts for sales promotion, corporate gifts, fund-raising, or educational purposes. Special editions can also be created to specifications. For details, contact the Special Sales Department, Sports Publishing, 307 West 36th Street, 11th Floor, New York, NY 10018 or sportspubbooks@skyhorsepublishing.com.

Sports Publishing® is a registered trademark of Skyhorse Publishing, Inc.®, a Delaware corporation.

Visit our website at www.sportspubbooks.com.

10 9 8 7 6 5 4 3 2 1

Library of Congress Cataloging-in-Publication Data is available on file.

Cover design by David Ter-Avanesyan
Cover images by Getty Images

ISBN: 978-1-68358-434-6
Ebook ISBN: 978-1-68358-441-4

Printed in the United States of America

DEDICATION

To my family: wife Nancy, sons Sean and Scott, daughters-in-law Rachel and Katie, and my grandson Nathan.

Also to my cousin Dale Stewart, a rugged fullback out of Carnegie Tech who is as comfortable with his artist's palette as he was with the pigskin.

And to four of my former colleagues in eduction, Karen Calloway, Susan Smith, Cathy Burchell, and Bonnie Glasbrenner.

ACKNOWLEDGMENTS

Thanks to my grandson, Nathan Stewart, for providing me with some material for this book—he deserves some "co-writing" acknowledgment!

CONTENTS

INTRODUCTION: GROUND RULES

Just as managers and umpires go over the ground rules prior to games, you need to understand how to use this book. Each chapter has questions of four levels of difficulty sprinkled throughout. Each question has an indication of what correct answers earn for you in terms of baseball, from a single for the easiest items to a home run for the toughest of questions.

Someone once said that in theory, a baseball game, played, of course, with no clock, could last infinitely. In fact, if hitters could manage an unending stream of hits, one inning could last indefinitely. Likewise, in this book, as long as you answer questions correctly, you'll rack up tons of hits and runs. Keep track as you progress through the book. After three outs—that is to say three incorrect answers—you end an inning and clear the bases of any runners you've earned before moving on to your next three outs. Compete against yourself or others and see just how many runs you can compile before making your 27th out.

All of the records and statistics used in this book are from the time period of 1900 through the 2020 season. In addition, when sources varied concerning records or stats, this book went with baseball-reference.com as the definitive source.

Admittedly, the determination of what each question

is worth is subjective, but we've tried to be fair in judging each question's difficulty. Also, you may notice there are fewer questions worth triples than other hits, but three-base hits are, in real life, quite rare. Overall, though, there was no deliberate attempt to have the ratio of the questions worth singles, doubles, triples, and homers reflect real baseball. After all, too many questions worth singles would make this book too easy, and having a ton of highly challenging questions with a home-run value to reflect the glut of players swinging for homers in the game in recent years, may have made the book ridiculously difficult for some readers.

Very few of the home-run questions were designed to baffle serious trivia buffs by asking about extremely obscure players, incidents, statistics, and records. However, if you come across a few that seem way too difficult, just imagine you're facing an overpowering pitcher and that you've decided to either swing from your heels and take a hack at such questions, or figuratively take three strikes and head back to the dugout. Look at it this way, even if you miss a few very tough ones, you'll probably learn something new and improve your game. In any event, just have fun.

One goal of the book was to supply the reader with a wide variety of questions. If you come across, say, several questions in a row dealing with a certain theme or topic, and you don't particularly care for that group of items, move on—there are many different types of questions to challenge and appeal to you. Again, read this book to entertain, to learn new facts, to be challenged, and to simply experience enjoyment.

All petty points and lead-in material aside, it's time to move on—it's your turn at the plate.

CHAPTER ONE
POSITION PLAYERS

1. Single: Which player dominated MVP voting for years, starting with his first full season when he came in second in the balloting? Through 2020, over his first nine full seasons, he won the trophy three times, finished second in the voting four times, came in fourth once, and wound up fifth in the balloting once as well. Therefore, he had been in the top five every season from 2012 through 2020, truly a remarkable streak.

2. Home Run: Many experts have argued about which trades are the worst in baseball history. One has to be the time (December of 1971) when the New York Mets gave up on a young Nolan Ryan, a pitcher who, after leaving the Mets, would go on to set a slew of records over his illustrious Hall of Fame career. Which infielder was traded by the California Angels to New York for the Ryan Express? It should also be noted that the Mets even threw in *three other players* in the deal!

3. Single: The 2020 season, almost decimated by COVID-19, limped its way to a conclusion with teams playing far fewer than the normal 162-game schedule. Nevertheless, some players still turned in shining performances. Which Dodger led the National League in

WAR? Clue: he was the American League MVP in 2018 and gave a good run at winning that award in the National League in 2020, finishing second (albeit a rather distant second).

4. Double: When French Bordagaray was with Brooklyn, he once was tagged out at the plate when he tried to score standing up. Asked why he hadn't slid, he stated that sliding might have meant he would have broken his cigars in his pocket. Now, which player who led his league in steals from 1981–1984 once shied away from sliding on his hips, choosing to go into bases headfirst because his hip pocket was where he stashed a vial of cocaine?

5. Double: One of the great early era stars amassed 914 stolen bases (no. 3 lifetime) from 1888 through 1901. In 2013, a rookie who had the same name as the speedster from long ago burst onto the scene. A statistical oddity: beginning in 2014, and over his first four full seasons the man in question stole 56, 57, 58, then 59 bases for the Cincinnati Reds. He was successful on 81 percent of his first 376 theft attempts. Name him.

6. Double: Among men who played 20+ years, who has the highest stolen-base percentage ever at 86.4 percent? a. Tim Raines b. Rickey Henderson c. Carlos Beltran d. Joe Morgan

7. Single: A rookie with the Reds in 2008, this powerful right fielder twice finished in the top 10 for MVP voting. Sometimes when he strolled into the batter's box, fans would drag out his last name, "Bruuuce." What's his first name?

8. Double: Who was the Orioles slugger who had a first name (actually, his nickname) that home fans loved to drag out? In his case, the collective cheer actually sounded like booing.

9. Single: Through 2020, this minor leaguer had yet to make his big-league debut—not even a cup of coffee for the man who, due to his having won a Heisman Trophy, was the biggest name in the minors since his first appearance there in 2016. His pro career .223 batting average didn't help. Like Michael Jordan, this man was proof that hitting a baseball was no easy task. Before the 2021 season, he decided to retire from baseball.

10. Single: Name the Dodger who stirred up controversy when, right after L.A. won the 2020 World Series, celebrated with teammates—at times without a mask—despite being aware that he had tested positive for the coronavirus.

11. Double: In the deciding Game Six of the 1995 ALCS, this Cleveland greyhound streaked all the way from second base to score on a passed ball, taking advantage of Seattle's Randy Johnson, who appeared to be distracted and upset by the misplay.

12. Single: From 1949 through 2020, only five players collected 100+ extra-base hits in a season. Three of them have been strongly accused of using performance-enhancing drugs, another played in a ballpark that helped hitters enormously, and the final one was a Diamondback. Name two of these men.

13. Double: In 1992, which Cleveland Indian became the second second baseman ever to hit .300 or higher while also collecting 200+ hits, 30+ doubles, 20 or more homers, and 100+ RBIs in a season?

14. Single: Who was the *first* second sacker to do this—and he did it five times in the 1920s?

15. Triple: During a Cleveland vs. Milwaukee game in 1996, the muscular 230-pound Albert Belle broke up a double play by smashing the Brewers' 170-pound second baseman with a vicious forearm shot. Who was the defender?

16. Single: In 2021, who signed a contract with a West Coast club that called for his getting paid $340 million over 14 seasons, making it the longest deal in baseball history?

17. Single: Prior to that contract, the two longest contracts belonged to a Marlin, who was traded a few years after signing a 13-year deal in November of 2014, and to a Philadelphia slugger whose 13-year deal was finalized before the 2019 season began. Name either man.

18. Single: What man played more games with the Orioles than any other player? Stretch this into a double if you can name two of the next three men on that list.

19. Single: Name the Phillies' leading or second leading player for most games played.

20. Single: Most games played by a Cub? Give yourself a double if you name two of the next three men on that list.

21. Single: Who is the Reds' leader for games played? Go for a double by identifying two of the next three players.

22. Single: In the 2015 NLDS, this man couldn't buy a hit, striking out in eight of his 17 plate appearances and batting .188. In the next year's Division Series he hit lower, at .130. In the 2017 World Series he hit .222 followed by a .150 batting average and a .143 in two subsequent postseason rounds. However, in the final three rounds of playoff action in 2020, he erupted, hitting .364, .310, and .400 in the World Series. He was named the MVP in the NLCS and World Series that year. Name this Dodger.

23. Single: Name the first or second switch-hitter to reach the 3,000 hit level.

24. Single: Although this 1985 MVP played his whole career (1982–1995) with the Yankees, he only played in the postseason once, his final season. He led the AL in doubles three times, averaging close to 50 per year.

25. Triple: What outfielder who played for the Twins for his first six seasons, then signed with the Indians and finished the 2021 season with the Braves, hitting a home run on the very first pitch he saw in the majors in 2015? He also homered during his first postseason at bat.

26. Single: Two New York ballplayers own their league records for hitting the most homers as a rookie player. Name the Met who, with 53 in 2019, hit one more than his AL counterpart.

27. Single: Name the Yankee who holds the AL rookie record with 52 HRs in 2017.

28. Double: Through 2020, only four other rookies have led their league in homers. Name one.

29. Double: What big-name player was a member of the World Champion team in 2019, then opted out of the 2020 season due to his concerns about COVID-19?

30. Single: True or false—Kirk Gibson won an MVP Award but he never was an All-Star.

31. Single: Fans easily recall Gibson smashing his 1988 World Series Game One home run, but how many plate appearances did he have in that Series? a. one b. six c. 15 d. 21

32. Single: In 2018, this Washington outfielder came in second in the Rookie of the Year voting. In his sophomore season, he cracked 34 HRs while scoring and driving in 110 runs. He had three homers in the 2019 World Series. Name him.

33. Double: Pitcher "Sad" Sam Jones had the habit of taking to the mound with a toothpick in his mouth. Years after he retired, another player, a shortstop mainly for the Royals, also played with a toothpick jammed into the corner of his mouth. Who is he?

34. Single: Name the Red Sox third baseman who led the AL with 54 doubles and 359 total bases in 2019.

35. Double: In 2019, which Dodger played every position on the diamond in at least one game with the exception of pitching (which he had done once the year before), designated hitter (which he had also done before), and catcher?

36. Double: Who was the Tampa Bay player who only had three total at-bats in the 2020 World Series, but he made one appearance really count, coming through with the key single in the bottom half of the ninth inning of Game Four? Two errors took place on the same play, allowing the Rays to win.

37. Single: On the play mentioned above, the line-drive single tied the game, and the winning run scored when the Dodgers made two errors—one by center fielder Chris Taylor and the other by the catcher, Will Smith. Which Ray, after stumbling, falling, getting back on his feet, and then, realizing the throw to the plate had him dead to rights, came to a full stop well shy of home plate, still managed to score the winning run?

38. Single: After winning the AL batting crown in

1967 with a .326 batting average, that statistic fell off 25 points for this outfielder. Still, his .301 mark led the league, but it remains the lowest batting average ever to win the crown. Who is this player?

39. Single: Who is the last man to win a Triple Crown, doing so in 2012 for an AL team?

40. Single: Through 2020, who was the last NL player to win back-to-back MVP Awards?

41. Single: Through 2020, who was the very last man to win consecutive MVP trophies?

42. Double: The next several questions share the theme of speed on the base paths. For many decades Ty Cobb monopolized stolen-base records. His single-season high water mark was 96 steals set in 1915, and that stood as the record until what man came along and swiped 104 in 1962?

43. Single: After the player referred to in the previous question, who was the next mercurial runner to hold the single-season steals record?

44. Single: Who broke the record mentioned above and still is the record holder for steals in a season? You can stretch this hit into a double if you can guess within five how many bases he stole.

45. Single: Back to Cobb. Not counting Hall of Famer Billy Hamilton, who by far played the bulk of his career before the dawn of the modern era (and stole 100 or more bases four times), two men eventually eclipsed Cobb's lifetime record for steals. Name both.

46. Single: Who holds the record for the most times being caught stealing during a season?

47. Double: Only two modern-era players ever stole 100+ bases three times. One was Rickey Henderson, whose three highest stolen-base totals came in 1980, 1982, and 1983. Who was the other man to achieve this feat?

48. Single: The 1970 AL Rookie of the Year tragically passed away in August of 1979 when, just a few seasons away from having won the MVP trophy, he was involved in an accident. Name this player who tied a World Series record when he belted hits in six straight Series at-bats.

49. Single: Who is, in fact, the only player other than Lou Gehrig to be inducted into the Hall of Fame without having to wait the required five years?

50. Double: Name either of the two hitters who rank no. 4 and no. 6 on the all-time list of highest lifetime batting averages. Clues: neither is in the Hall of Fame. One, despite hitting .356 for his career, never made it to Cooperstown due to a scandal; the other man missed out on Hall of Fame status due to factors such as his short big-league career (11 seasons) and, consequently, some low lifetime statistics such as his hitting only 113 home runs and driving in just 542 runs. Still, with a .349 lifetime batting average, it's clear that this man could hit.

51. Single: Through 2020, who was the last player in the majors to stay with just one team for a career that lasted at least a dozen seasons? Clue: he played in the infield for the Boston Red Sox for 14 years until 2020 when, hurt, he did not play a single game.

52. Double: What team did Carlos Beltran begin his big-league career with?

53. Single: In 2007, with which team did Hunter Pence break into the majors?

54. Single: Kirk Gibson's most memorable accomplishment is associated with the Dodgers, but with which team did he make his debut?

55. Double: Switching gears a bit, which was the last big-league club that the 1997 Rookie of the Year Scott Rolen played for?

56. Double: With which team did Joe Torre conclude his 18-year career as a player in the majors?

57. Double: What was the last club for Julio Franco, who endured for 23 seasons and didn't hang up his spikes in the majors until he was had become a baseball Methuselah at the age of 49?

58. Double: Who was the youngest man ever to win a batting crown, winning his only one in 1955 for an AL team?

59. Single: Who was the youngest player to win a batting title in the NL? a. Pete Reiser b. Juan Soto c. Barry Larkin d. Pete Rose

60. Double: Who was the first rookie ever to win his league's batting title, accomplishing this with his .323 average in 1964 for an AL team?

61. Single: Who is the only other modern-era rookie to win a batting crown? Clue: he did this at the age of 27, having tons of pro experience elsewhere.

62. Single: Name this star from the clues given—he played in 40 games in 2011, but his official rookie season was 2012 when he led his league in runs with 129 and stolen bases with 49. He also swatted 30 homers, allowing him to join the 30 homers/30 steals club, and he drove home 83 runs. He did all of this even though he wasn't on the big-league roster out of spring training, and he didn't play in his first game that season until April 28.

63. Double: Name the player who experts say is the only man to be thrown out at first base by the left fielder after seemingly ripping a single to that field. Clue: the batter in question was nicknamed The Mayor.

64. Single: In 2021, a catcher made history by making

his 17th successive Opening Day start, all with the same club. Who is this durable, valuable receiver?

65. Triple: In 2018, a catcher broke in with the Tigers and tied a record of sorts as, at the height of 6'6", the tallest catcher ever in the majors. Name this player.

66. Double: What mercurial center fielder who starred primarily for Cleveland, but spent time with 11 clubs in all, had been a point guard for the Arizona Wildcats who lost in the Elite Eight of the NCAA tournament to UNLV by one point in March 1989?

67. Single: A famous play cost the Boston Red Sox Game Six of the 1986 World Series when a 10th-inning groundball went through the legs of their first baseman, Bill Buckner, allowing the game-winning run to score. Who became a part of baseball history by hitting the dribbler?

68. Home Run: This may be an easy one for Mets fans, but it's rather difficult for most fans: who scored the winning run on the misplay of the easy grounder?

69. Double: Like Buckner, a Cubs first baseman also came up empty on a routine groundball. His came in a playoff game in 1984 against the San Diego Padres. The Cubs had made postseason play for the first time since 1945, but they were denied a trip to the World Series due to a groundball off the bat of Tim Flannery which trickled through the legs of their first baseman. Can you identify that player?

70. Double: Everyone recognizes the jersey numbers of famous players such as Hank Aaron with his familiar no. 44, but many stars didn't always wear the number that became synonymous with them. Start with Aaron—what was his uniform number during his rookie year of 1954? a. 3 b. 5 c. 22 d. he wore both 3 and 5 that season.

71. Double: What number did Joe DiMaggio wear on his pinstriped jersey when he first broke into the majors? a. 1 b. 7 c. 9 d. 13

72. Double: How about Mickey Mantle? What was his uniform number when he cracked the Yankees lineup as a member of the AL rookie crop of 1951? a. 6 b. 7 c. 10 d. 44

73. Double: Time for more uniform numbers with basic math thrown in. Add the jersey numbers (the ones most associated with the players in question) together and provide the grand total of those numbers. Begin with Babe Ruth plus Lou Gehrig added together with the number worn by Yogi Berra.

74. Triple: Start with Mike Trout's jersey number, and then subtract the number worn by Fernando Tatis Jr. Finally, add in Willie McCovey's uniform number.

75. Double: Start with Freddie Freeman's number. Add in Chipper Jones's jersey number. Now multiply the sum by the number worn on the back of Ozzie Smith.

76. Triple: Who holds the record for the most runs

driven in during a season by a leadoff hitter with 103? He accomplished this with the Colorado Rockies.

77. Double: Who was the first switch-hitter to amass 100 or more hits batting lefty and 100+ hitting righty? This shortstop did this in 1979 when he was with the St. Louis Cardinals.

78. Single: In December of 1981, the player from the previous question was traded to a West Coast team for another shortstop—name him.

79. Single: One year after the first player was able to bang out 100+ hits from both sides of the plate, this man just nearly matched him, with 99 hits. Name the AL speedster (he had 79 steals in 1980) who did this.

80. Double: What dynamic player, most known for being a part of the St. Louis Cardinals Gashouse Gang, was apparently done with his play in the majors in 1940 (he continued to play and manage in the minors)? Then, due to the World War II shortage of major-league manpower, he resumed his career with the Cards in 1944 for 40 games at the age of 40.

81. Double: That shortage also led to a one-armed outfielder becoming a big-leaguer. He became a part of baseball lore when he played for the St. Louis Browns in 1945, hitting .218 in his only major-league season.

82. Single: Born in Las Vegas, and fittingly a graduate of Bonanza High School in Vegas, this third baseman won the 2015 Rookie of the Year Award then proved there was no luck involved by winning the NL MVP the following season.

83. Single: He's played for the Astros when he broke into the majors in 2011, the Tigers, the Diamondbacks, and the Red Sox. In his first season with Boston he led the league with 130 RBIs—name him.

84. Double: Name the Gold Glove–winning first baseman who led the NL in getting plunked by pitches in 2015, 2017, and 2019.

85. Double: Two Houston Astros launched deep drives that struck seats in the Astrodome's fourth deck. To commemorate those feats, the team painted the seats. Due to the men's nicknames, one player had a rooster painted on "his" seat; the other a cannon.

86. Double: What player, listed at 5'10" and 185 pounds, had the nickname Penguin when he played for the Dodgers, Cubs, and in 1987 for the A's?

87. Double: What player earned the nickname The Human Rain Delay because he took so long, going through all kinds of preparatory moves, before he settled in the box?

88. Single: What slugger was nicknamed Crime Dog because his last name sounded much like the name of a cartoon dog, the one known for the line "take a bite out of crime"?

89. Single: Great catchers have been around forever with men such as Bill Dickey, Roy Campanella, Yogi Berra, Johnny Bench, and Ivan Rodriguez mentioned among the very best. See if you can name this catcher—from his rookie season of 2004 through 2020, his team, with him usually behind the plate, was tops at giving up the least amount of stolen bases (847). The number two team in that department surrendered over 400 more steals (1,250). Not only that, but only 519 of the 847 steals his team gave up came with the man in question catching, and that came over a stretch of 1,989 games, meaning in all the other games from that time frame, 501 games in all, his backup catchers allowed 328 steals. Who is this superlative catcher?

90. Double: Who is the oldest player to ever hit a home run?

91. Triple: Who is the oldest player to ever bash a grand slam?

92. Double: Who was the first man to drill 30+ homers in the same season he stole 30 or more bases? a. Ken Williams b. Rogers Hornsby c. Willie Mays d. Hank Aaron

93. Triple: Two men share the record for hitting the most homers, five, in a double header. Name either man.

94. Double: Two first basemen were nicknamed the Big Cat. Name either one of these power hitters.

95. Single: Who was the fastest second baseman to reach the 100-home-run mark? a. Alfonso Soriano b. Dan Uggla c. Ryne Sandberg d. Joe Morgan

96. Double: The 1930 season was called the Year of the Rabbit Ball because the baseball was said to be so lively it flew off bats with, by pitchers' reckoning, alarming regularity. Someone said if you held a baseball up to your ear back then, you could hear the rapid thumping of a rabbit's heartbeat. Your question: what fireplug of a man, a future Hall of Famer, set the all-time record that season by driving in 191 runs?

97. Double: 1930 was also the season in which a player hit .386 with 40 HRs and 170 RBIs yet did not lead his league in any of those categories—name this Phillies outfielder.

98. Double: Through 2020, who was the last man to win both a Rookie of the Year and an MVP Award? He was a rookie in 2014 and won his MVP Award in 2020.

99. Single: Christian Yelich won the 2018 NL MVP, but who did he break into the majors with in 2013?

100. Single: Bobby Grich, a six-time All-Star, split his 17-year career between which two clubs?

101. Double: Cal Ripken Jr. was the Orioles' everyday shortstop from 1983 to 1996, and we mean *every* single day for the durable Ripken (who did play six games at third base in 1996). Who became Baltimore's regular shortstop in 1997?

102. Double: Who holds the record for hitting the most homers in his final big-league season?

103. Triple: Who held the record before the player mentioned above broke it? Clue: a controversial figure, this man played for seven teams over 16 major-league seasons from 1971 to 1986.

104. Single: Which NL star smacked 30 or more doubles and homers, drove in 100+ runs, and hit .300 or better every year from his rookie season of 2001 through 2010?

105. Double: Name either man who shares the record for the most grand slams hit in a season. Clues: both did this as AL players, one with the New York Yankees, the other with the Cleveland Indians.

106. Triple: Who is the only man to hit two grand slams in the same inning?

107. Single: Which Boston Red Sox player was the first man to win the MVP Award in his rookie season?

108. Home Run: Who owns the highest batting average ever for a rookie?

109. Single: Who holds the record for the most hits in a season?

110. Triple: Who held the single-season hit record before the man from the previous question came along?

111. Double: Who, in 2001, established a record for the most RBIs by a NL rookie?

112. Double: Which AL legend holds the overall mark for the most runs driven home by a rookie?

113. Double: Who holds the record for the most hits produced in a rookie season?

114. Home Run: Whose ancient record did the man from the above question beat?

CHAPTER ONE ANSWERS: POSITION PLAYERS

1. Mike Trout

2. Jim Fregosi, a six-time All-Star. He was a very solid player, but one who hit just .232 and .234 in his short stint, a mere two years and 146 games, with the Mets. Meanwhile, during Ryan's first three years with California, he averaged 21 wins per season. Furthermore, the first year after the transaction, Ryan led the American League in strikeouts with a whopping 329 K's. This was the first of seven strikeout crowns he won for the Angels over an eight-year span. The all-time strikeout king would cop four more K crowns late in his career with Houston and Texas.

Final note and an explanation as to why the Mets gave up on Ryan: first of all, for years they had tried to plug a hole at third base with a proven talent, so they were desperate to get Fregosi, who they believed was finally the man to fill the bill at the hot corner; secondly, Ryan only had a record of 29–38 with the Mets—but he would go on to win almost exactly 300 more games over his 27-year career.

3. The multi-talented Mookie Betts

4. Tim Raines, who went on to become a Hall of Famer

5. Billy Hamilton

6. c. Beltran. While he stole only 312 bases compared to, for example, 689 for Morgan and 808 for Raines, he had a great success rate.

7. Jay [Bruce]

8. Boog Powell. The 1970 MVP rarely heard actual boos.

9. Tim Tebow. He was the first sophomore to win the Heisman (2007).

10. Justin Turner. He had left the final game of the Series in the eighth inning and he spent the last two innings in a doctor's office close to the clubhouse. However, he joined his teammates, hugging them on the field after the win.

11. Kenny Lofton. This play helped propel Cleveland into the World Series. Some of the blame for his scoring may belong to catcher Dan Wilson, who seemed to think there was no way Lofton could advance 180 feet on the play.

12. Barry Bonds, Sammy Sosa, Albert Belle, Todd Helton (in consecutive years, a first), and Luis Gonzalez

13. Carlos Baerga. He was also the first man to hit home runs batting lefty and righty in the same inning.

14. Rogers Hornsby, a career .358 hitter. In his best season, 1922, his numbers were insane: 250 hits, 46 doubles, 42 homers, 152 RBIs, and, to top off his 1922 Triple Crown, he hit .401. As if that's not enough, he won another Triple Crown three seasons later when he hit .403 to go with his 41 two-base hits, 39 home runs, and 143 runs driven in.

He truly was a hitting juggernaut. For example, from 1920–1924, he averaged 42 doubles per year and led the NL in that category four times. He also averaged 15 triples each year while leading the league once, and he was first in the NL in homers twice over that span. In addition, he once enjoyed a six-year period in which he led the league in ribbies four times. Finally, over a jaw-dropping five-year stretch he averaged hitting .402. Hitting .400 is nearly impossible, yet he averaged that for half a decade!

15. Fernando Vina

16. Fernando Tatis Jr.

17. Giancarlo Stanton and Bryce Harper

18. Cal Ripken Jr. followed by Brooks Robinson, Mark Belanger, and Eddie Murray

19. Mike Schmidt is first, then Jimmy Rollins.

20. Ernie Banks followed by Cap Anson, Billy Williams, and Ryne Sandberg

21. Pete Rose ranks first. Next: Dave Concepcion, Barry Larkin, and Johnny Bench.

22. Corey Seager

23. Pete Rose was first, then Eddie Murray.

24. Don Mattingly, a.k.a. Donnie Baseball

25. Eddie Rosario

26. Pete Alonso, the sixth Met to win the Rookie of the Year Award

27. Aaron Judge

28. Mark McGwire, Ralph Kiner, Tim Jordan (but with

POSITION PLAYERS • 23

only 12 homers in 1906), and Harry Lumley (who hit a mere nine in 1904)

29. Ryan Zimmerman

30. True

31. a. one

32. Juan Soto

33. UL Washington—the "UL" is his real first name, not his initials. It's said that as a youth he played with a blade of grass in his mouth, but when he became a Royal and played on artificial turf, with no grass in sight, he substituted toothpicks.

34. Rafael Devers

35. Kike Hernandez

36. Brett Phillips, who celebrated the win by racing around with arms extended not unlike a child pretending to be an airplane. The two errors on the same play were the only two of the entire contest.

37. Randy Arozarena

38. Carl Yastrzemski. 1968 was a bizarre year in baseball, often referred to as the Year of the Pitcher. It was a season filled with minuscule ERAs and position players' batting averages to match. For example, the average

ERA for all AL pitchers was 2.98, and AL hitters could muster only a .230 batting average.

39. Miguel Cabrera of the Tigers. His statistics: 44 HRs, 139 RBIs, and a batting average of .330. He easily won the MVP Award that season, and quite a few of his 2013 season stats were almost exact mirror images of his Triple Crown season as he again hit 44 homers, drove in 137 runs, and upped his batting average to .348.

40. Albert Pujols won his consecutive MVPs in 2008 and 2009 with the Cardinals.

41. Miguel Cabrera. His back-to-back MVP trophies were won in 2012 and 2013.

42. Maury Wills of the Dodgers. Wills led the league in stolen bases six straight seasons from 1960 through 1965 (but never again). For the record, and this is something many trivia buffs find a bit surprising, Cobb only led his league in steals six times over his 24-year career.

43. Lou Brock of the Cardinals pilfered 118 bases in 1974.

44. The current record holder is Rickey Henderson and, with 130 SBs to his credit in 1982 (when he was 23 years old), his hold on this mark seems very secure. This speed burner led his league in stolen bases seven years in a row and a dozen seasons in all. He was 39 years old when he topped the AL in this department for the last time.

45. Brock was the first to ease by Cobb's 897 career steals. Henderson followed, but he blew by everyone, ending up with 1,406 SBs to 938 for Brock.

46. Henderson in 1982. That season he attempted a total of 172 bases—that's a whole lot of running. While he did set the record that season with his 130 steals, he also established the record for the most times caught stealing, 42.

It seems quite logical that he also holds the lifetime record for being caught stealing at 335 over his 25 big-league seasons. Still, that's not too bad at all when you consider Brock, who had almost 500 fewer steals than the dynamic Henderson, was caught 307 times. Plus, Henderson's success rate for base burglary was a superb 81 percent, and he was still able to swipe as many as 31 bases at the age of 41 and 25 more the next year.

47. Vince Coleman. Amazingly, his three seasons with 100 or more steals came in his *first three major-league seasons*. He was the Rookie of the Year in 1985 when he set a personal high of 110 steals, and he followed that up by stealing 107 and 109 the following two seasons. Not only that, he led the NL in steals for six successive seasons, 1985–1990.

48. Thurman Munson. He came through big time in postseason play, hitting .357 for his 135 plate appearances. He hit even higher for his 72 plate appearances during World Series play at .373. After he died in a plane crash at the age of 32, there was talk of immediately waiving the five-year waiting period, as had been done with Lou Gehrig, and electing Munson into the Hall of Fame. The Baseball Writers Association of America decided to allow him to be on the ballot in 1981, a few years before the waiting period would have transpired, but he only garnered 15.5 percent of the votes and never again received more than 9.5 percent of the votes cast. Therefore, emotions and a fine career aside, he never made it to Cooperstown.

49. Roberto Clemente. Like Munson, Clemente was a victim of an airplane crash, but the sentiment to quickly allow him into the Hall of Fame was strong, as were his lifetime statistics. Clemente passed away on December 31, 1972, and he was voted into the Hall in 1973 by a special election.

50. The .356 hitter is Shoeless Joe Jackson, while the other player from this question is Lefty O'Doul.

51. Dustin Pedroia. He made his official retirement announcement in February of 2021.

52. The Kansas City Royals. He played in just 14 games in 1998, but the next season he was the Rookie of the Year. He would go on to play for seven teams over his 20 years in the majors.

53. Pence started out with the Houston Astros, but spent more seasons with the Giants. He also suited up for the Phillies and Rangers.

54. Gibson began with the Tigers in 1979, having

earlier been a baseball and football star at Michigan State University. Although many fans have forgotten this, he also played one season each for two teams, the Royals and Pirates.

55. Rolen ended his 17-year stay in the majors with the Cincinnati Reds, playing there in his final four seasons after playing well for the Phillies, the Cardinals, then briefly with the Blue Jays.

56. Torre wrapped things up as a Met in 1977. Well-versed trivia lovers know just how good he was as a player for the Braves and Cardinals, too. He was a nine-time All-Star who won the NL MVP Award in 1971 when he hit a lofty .363—and as a very slow runner, very few if any of his league-leading 230 hits were extra-base hits.

57. Franco's last *big-league* team was Atlanta. He also played for teams in Japan, Mexico, and Korea. Franco, who has a batting crown to his credit (he hit .341 in 1991), was a true baseball vagabond having also played for the Indians, Rangers, Mets, Devil Rays, Phillies, White Sox, and Brewers.

58. Al Kaline. He broke the record held by another Detroit Tiger, Ty Cobb. Kaline hit .340 to win his crown at the age of 20 even though he was in his third season—he played in 30 then 138 games during his first couple of seasons. Kaline was just 12 days younger than Cobb when the Georgia Peach won his first batting title.

59. Take credit for either a. Reiser or b. Soto. In the very abbreviated 2020 season, Soto did lead his league with a .351 batting average, albeit with only 196 plate appearances. He did not hit his 21st birthday until a month after the end of the 2020 season. Reiser hit .343 in his first full season of 1941 for the Brooklyn Dodgers, doing so with 601 plate appearances, a true test of time. He turned 22 shortly before the 1941 season began. Larkin never won a batting title and Rose was 27 before he took home his first of three batting crowns.

60. Tony Oliva. Naturally, he was rewarded with a Rookie of the Year Award. It didn't hurt his cause that he also led the AL in runs, hits, and doubles. His overall stats declined a bit in 1965, but he won another batting title (his second of three), showing consistency by hitting .321 and guiding his Twins to a pennant.

61. In 2001, Seattle's Ichiro Suzuki, having been purchased from the Japanese major leagues, hit .350 to win the AL batting title.

Here's an absolutely unbelievable bit of trivia—one writer from a Cleveland suburb's newspaper gave his first-place vote to Indians pitcher CC Sabathia, preventing Ichiro from being an unanimous choice for the Rookie of the Year Award. Sabathia did win 17 games, but his ERA was a bit high at 4.39 and his WHIP stood at 1.353, nothing spectacular. Meanwhile, Ichiro led the AL in hits with 242, steals with 56, and he ripped 34 doubles on his way to winning the MVP. So he was good enough to be the MVP, but not worthy of a first-place vote by one writer for Rookie of the Year.

Here's what's more unfathomable, and much worse. The writer said he did not consider Ichiro, who did have tons of experience in pro ball in Japan, to be a rookie, so he could not be the Rookie of the Year. However, that writer cast his second-place vote for Rookie of the Year to…Ichiro, the man he said *wasn't* a rookie. Not a rookie, but his choice as that year's second best *rookie*! The official rules said Ichiro was, in fact, a major-league rookie that year, so it wasn't the writer's place to use his "logic" to deny Ichiro unanimous status.

62. Mike Trout

63. Sean Casey. When he was with the Detroit Tigers in 2006, he hit a ball that ticked the glove of the White Sox third baseman Joe Crede and into left field. Casey started out of the batter's box, but then, thinking he saw the baseball being snagged by the leaping Crede, came to a halt. Finally, too late it turns out, he took off again for first base. Meanwhile, left fielder Pablo Ozuna charged in, bare-handed the ball in shallow left field, and fired all the way to first to nip Casey for a strange 5-to-7-to-3 assist/putout. One estimate had Casey's belated journey to the bag taking about eight seconds.

64. Yadier Molina of the St. Louis Cardinals

65. Grayson Greiner, who *really* has to hunker down to give his pitchers low targets

66. Kenny Lofton. He was a Wildcat teammate of Sean

Elliott and Anthony Cook, and he averaged 4.1 assists per game for his senior season.

67. Mookie Wilson. Buckner should never have had to shoulder all of the blame for the tough loss. The Red Sox bullpen should share some of the responsibility for giving this one away. Two relievers failed to protect a 5–3 lead in the tenth inning even after the first two Mets were retired.

68. Ray Knight

69. Leon Durham, who giveth to the Cubs with a two-run homer to open the scoring in the top of the first in the deciding game of the NLCS, but who also taketh away when he made his egregious error on an easy play. San Diego entered the seventh inning down, 3–2, but Durham's error opened the door and the Padres wound up putting a four spot on the board to close out the game's scoring.

70. b. Aaron wore no. 5 as a rookie.

71. c. In 1936, DiMaggio (like his rival Ted Williams would wear) had no. 9 on the back of his shirt.

72. a. Mantle wore no. 6 before he upped it to his famous no. 7 later that season.

73. The sum of those numbers is 15. Ruth's no. 3 plus Gehrig's no. 4 added to Berra's no. 8 gives you 15.

74. Trout's number is 27. Tatis Jr. gives you the number 23. So the first part of the question results in four. Add McCovey's 44 for the answer of 48.

75. Freeman's number is 5. Jones wore no. 10. Smith carried the number 1 on his back. The solution to this math problem is 15.

76. Charlie Blackmon. In 2017, the All-Star center fielder broke Darin Erstad's record of 100 RBIs from the leadoff spot set 17 years earlier.

77. Garry Templeton. He led the league that year with 211 hits, but he had to scramble down the stretch to record his 100th hit as a right-handed hitter. He wound up batting righty even against right-handed pitchers over his final seven games.

78. Ozzie Smith. Other players such as Sixto Lezcano were involved in the trade, but Smith, of course, turned out to be the key to this swap.

79. Willie Wilson. He ended the year with 230 hits in all to lead the AL, and it didn't hurt his cause that, like Templeton, he was his team's leadoff hitter. In his trivia-making season Templeton had 696 plate appearances, and Wilson had an even higher total with 745 plate appearances.

80. Pepper Martin, a lifetime .298 hitter who had a respectable .279 batting average in 1944

81. Pete Gray, who had stolen 68 bases, hit five homers, and batted .333 in his first season in pro ball, 1944

82. Kris Bryant

83. J.D. Martinez

84. Anthony Rizzo

85. The rooster was for Doug Rader, the Red Rooster. The cannon was for the Toy Cannon, Jimmy Wynn.

86. Ron Cey

87. Mike Hargrove

88. Fred McGriff. The dog's name was McGruff.

89. Yadier Molina. He permitted about one stolen base per every four games he played, while his backups allowed one steal for every game and a half. Another way to look at Molina's skill—if he had given up stolen bases at the same rate as his teammates, instead of allowing only 519 steals, he would have given up about 1,325 steals from 2004 through 2020!

90. Julio Franco. He set the current record with his first (and only) home run of his final big-league season (2007) when he was 48 years, eight months, and 11 days old. He had previously broken the former record held by pitcher Jack Quinn when he hit a pinch homer on April 20, 2006.

91. Franco again. His record-setting grand slam came in 2005. He was 46 years old at the time (pushing 47), breaking his own record that he first established in 2004.

92. a. Ken Williams in 1922. No other player would join the 30/30 club until 1956, when Mays hit 36 HRs with 40 SBs. This feat was still pretty rare until around 1987. From 1922 until 1990, the 30/30 plateaus were reached 17 times. Then, in the 1990s alone, players hit those levels 20 times.

93. Stan Musial and Nate Colbert. Colbert drove in 13 runs and set a twinbill record with 22 total bases on August 1, 1972. Interestingly, he hit his five homers off five different pitchers. Also, four of his blasts came on first pitches and, in all, it took him just six swings to collect his five home runs. In a remarkable coincidence, a young Colbert was in attendance when Musial went on his home-run binge and set a record with 21 total bases in one day. Musial's manager, Solly Hemus, said, "He acted like he did it everyday. That's just the way he was, very nonchalant about his accomplishments." Despite Musial's home-run heroics, his Cardinals could only muster a split of the doubleheader. Musial admitted that when he had an opportunity to hit a sixth home run he, uncharacteristically, tried to pulverize the ball. The result was a weak popup.

94. Johnny Mize and Andres Galarraga

95. a. Uggla, then with the Florida Marlins. He hit his 100th homer in his 502nd big-league contest, early in his fourth season. He averaged over 30 HRs per year for his first seven seasons. He hit 22 more the next year, then managed only four more home runs over the following two seasons before calling it quits.

96. Hack Wilson. He also set the NL high for homers with 56, a record that stood until the Steroid Era.

97. Chuck Klein, who is also the only man to win a Triple Crown then get traded the next season. The 1930 season was so wild, the composite batting average in the NL was .303, and, as a team, Klein's Phils hit .315 yet finished 40 games out of first, lodged in the cellar.

98. José Abreu

99. Miami. In his sophomore season he, Marcell Ozuna, and Giancarlo (Mike) Stanton gave the Marlins a pretty solid, up-and-coming starting outfield. By 2018, none of them would still be with Miami.

100. Grich broke in with the Baltimore Orioles and ended his career with the California Angels.

101. Mike Bordick who, at age 31, was five years younger than Ripken. Bordick went on to set records for the most consecutive games and most chances accepted without an error at shortstop.

102. David Ortiz. He was 40 years old in 2016 when he crushed 38 homers before retiring.

103. Dave Kingman. He hit 35 HRs in 1986 when he was a 37-year-old designated hitter with the Oakland Athletics.

104. Albert Pujols. He set the NL record for the most consecutive seasons (10) with 100+ runs driven in.

105. Don Mattingly (1987) and Travis Hafner (2006) both hit six grand slams in a season.

106. Fernando Tatis Sr. with the St. Louis Cardinals in 1999

107. Fred Lynn who, of course, was also the 1975 Rookie of the Year.

108. Shoeless Joe Jackson. He hit .408 in 1911 and even that wasn't good enough to give him the batting crown, as Ty Cobb checked in at .419.

109. Ichiro Suzuki, with 262 in 2004. He set the record during a 162-game schedule, playing in 161 contests.

110. George Sisler. He rapped 257 hits in 1920, playing in all 154 scheduled games. After Ichiro's 154th game, he had 251 hits, still shy of Sisler's record. Just as was the case when Roger Maris played his record-setting 1961 season which afforded him with eight games more than Babe Ruth had when he set his season homer record, Ichiro benefited from the luck of playing a longer season than Sisler.

Controversy raged about Maris topping Ruth, but here's an easy solution that could stop any debates: simply keep two columns of all records—one for marks set under the old 154-game setup, and another for records established during 162-game seasons. Of course, if anyone, for example, broke an old record, and did so during the year's first 154 games, then he would deserve to be listed in both columns as the undisputed record holder. Under this arrangement, Maris would have earned his place in the 162-game record column, while Ruth would still have received the credit he deserved for his stupendous feat.

111. Albert Pujols with 130. Trivia tidbit: In April of 2006, he set the NL record for the most homers hit in the month of April, 14. That same month, the Kansas City Royals, *as a team*, hit exactly 14 home runs. It took Pujols only 81 at-bats to reach his 14 HRs; it took the Royals 722 at-bats to match him!

112. Ted Williams. He drove in 145 as a rookie in 1939.

113. This is yet another record set by Ichiro. He collected 242 hits in 2001.

114. Shoeless Joe Jackson with 233 hits in 1911.

CHAPTER TWO
PITCHERS

1. Triple: When Pittsburgh Pirates star second base-man Bill Mazeroski crushed a high slider over the left-field wall in Forbes Field to dramatically end the 1960 World Series, he did so against a New York Yankee who was normally a starter. Just two years later the pitcher redeemed himself by helping the Yankees win the World Series, copping the Series MVP Award along the way. Which pitcher was this who experienced the ultimate highs and lows of World Series play?

2. Double: When Sandy Koufax threw his perfect game in 1965, his mound opponent Bob Hendley turned in a performance that wasn't too far from being perfect, either. How many hits did he give up? Give yourself a home run for this item if you can also tell how long his no-hitter held up (within one inning), *and* how many base runners he surrendered that game.

3. Home Run: Which pitcher who made it to the "Show" in 1981 with the Padres served up Pete Rose's record-setting 4,192nd hit to snap his tie with Ty Cobb?

4. Single: Which standout pitcher surrendered Alex Rodriguez's 3,000th hit? Clue: despite winning a Cy

Young Award and the MVP in the same season, he got a lot (disproportionate amount?) of attention for marrying Kate Upton.

5. Single: Many of the fastest pitches ever thrown in the majors came blistering off the left arm of a Cuban-born All-Star reliever who began his career with the Reds. Can you identify him?

6. Home Run: This 6'7" relief pitcher gained some fame as a college basketball player whose most famous North Carolina State teammate was David Thompson. He became the only man to win an NCAA hoop championship and a World Series title. Identify him.

7. Single: Name the AL pitcher who won the 2020 Cy Young Award while winning the Triple Crown of pitching.

8. Double: During a game in which replacement umpires were being used, a Cleveland pitcher felt the home plate ump had badly blown a call on a pitch. The pitcher marched to the plate, got a ball, and held it over home plate to show the ump that the pitch's location had clearly been where he was indicating, in the strike zone. Remarkably, the umpire did not eject this player. Clue: the Nicaraguan pitcher, nicknamed El Presidente, finished his career with 245 wins.

9. Single: Striking out 300 or more batters in a year is quite rare—it's only been done by 19 pitchers since 1901. Because Sandy Koufax's 382 strikeouts in 1965 set a since-broken record, this man's 325 K's in '65 had to settle for being second best in the majors that season.

10. Double: The largest single-season difference between a pitcher's ERA and his league's ERA is a record held by which Red Sox pitcher?

11. Double: Which Braves hurler holds that ERA disparity record for a NL pitcher?

12. Single: In 2015 this lefty won Pitcher of the Month three times for Houston. The year's Cy Young winner, he is the first man ever to go 15–0 in his home games over a season.

13. Home Run: One of the more obscure pitchers to throw a perfect game has the same first name as the answer to the previous question. He did this in 2010 with the A's. Name him.

14. Triple: During spring training of 1993 three Cleveland pitchers were involved in a boat accident that took the lives of two of those men. Name two of these pitchers.

15. Double: Twenty-three years later, another boating accident claimed the life of a Miami pitcher. In his four years in the majors he won 69 percent of his decisions and he had won 16 games through his September accident. Name him.

16. Single: True or false—Tom Seaver pitched his last

game as a Met in 1983, yet when he passed away in 2020, he was still the career team leader for wins, ERA, and strikeouts.

17. Home Run: A relief pitcher with Florida in 2000 when he led the league with 45 saves, this man was born with six fingers on each hand and six toes on each foot—who is he?

18. Double: A Hall of Fame right-handed hurler lost part of his right index finger due to a childhood accident involving a piece of farm equipment. That injury actually helped his pitching career as the baseball moved unnaturally on its way to the plate. His nickname is related to his pitching hand.

19. Single: Through the 2020 season, who was the last AL pitcher to win the MVP Award?

20. Single: Through 2020, who was the very last pitcher to win an MVP trophy?

21. Single: Coming off a Cy Young Award–winning season in 2020, which pitcher signed a contract that paid him $1.5 million more than the entire 26-man roster of the 2021 Pittsburgh Pirates?

22. Home Run: Who was the first pitcher ever to start an All-Star Game in both the NL and the AL?

23. Single: Steve Stone won nearly 80 percent of his decisions in 1980, the year he won the AL Cy Young

Award. He is said to have won his 25 games by sacrificing his arm, throwing an overabundance of hard curveballs. His arm shot, the next year he took a nose dive to a 4–7 record and his ERA soared from 3.23 to 4.60. That 1981 season was his last one in the majors. So, which team did Stone pitch for in his final three years in the majors?

24. Double: Dwight Gooden made a huge impact when he broke into the majors, but due to some serious issues, he faded by the end of his career. In his final season he suited up for three teams—which was the last major-league squad he played for?

25. Double: Southpaw Billy Wagner was only 5'10" and 180 pounds, but he could, as an old baseball expression goes, "throw a strawberry through a brick wall." Sure, Superman had the ability to leap tall buildings in a single bound, but Wagner had the ability to top 100 mph on his fastball—and he did that when that was still a very rare, highly noteworthy feat. An All-Star in Houston where he once finished fourth in Cy Young voting, like so many stars, he moved around, playing for five clubs in all. Which team was his last one in the majors? a. Mets b. Phillies c. Red Sox d. Braves

26. Home Run: Andrew Miller was only with Cleveland for three years, but under manager Terry Francona he helped change the way some managers used their bullpen. Early on during his career, he floundered—he once had a season ERA of 8.54 over nine games (seven as a starter). The first team he played for only kept him for two seasons, including 13 starts—he didn't find his niche in the bullpen until 2012 when he was with his third club, the Red Sox. So, with whom did he break into the majors?

27. Triple: Curtis Montague Schilling, better known as Curt, was drafted in 1986 by the Red Sox—the last club he played for. However, in 1988, he made his big-league debut. With which team was that?

28. Double: Southpaw Jerry Reuss was a star for more than 20 years, playing for eight teams, winning a personal high of 18 games on three occasions and a total of 220 wins. His longest stint was with the Dodgers, but with whom did he break in back in 1969?

29. Single: Now on to some questions about the last club a few select pitchers were with. Which team was standout reliever Rollie Fingers with when he retired in 1985?

30. Double: Jon Matlack was one of those pretty big-name pitchers who clearly had talent and quite a bit of value to his two teams. As a Met, he won the 1972 Rookie of the Year Award when he went 15–10. In seven of his 13 seasons he won in double figures, and he led the NL in shutouts twice. In December of 1977 he was involved in a whopping four-team trade that included 10 other players such as Bert Blyleven and Al Oliver. Who did Matlack wind up playing for from 1978 through the end of his career?

31. Home Run: Denny McLain is always remembered as the Detroit ace who won back-to-back Cy Young

Awards and, in 1968, not only won that award, but the MVP as well. After going 31-6 for a .838 winning percentage, that was hardly a surprise. However, he ran into some problems and by 1971 was a Tigers castoff, moving on to Washington where he won 10 games but dropped 22 decisions to lead the AL. Finally, in 1972, he spent time with two teams. Name either one.

32. Single: Fill in the blank with the name of a pitcher for the 1948 Boston Braves to complete a famous phrase that stemmed from the fact that the Braves, who won the pennant that year, relied heavily upon two of their starters for their success. "Spahn and ____, and pray for rain."

33. Double: Another team, the Angels, adopted a similar phrase which you must complete to earn your extra-base hit. "_____ and Ryan and two days of cryin'."

34. Home Run: In the first game of the 1966 World Series a relief pitcher set a record that has lasted for ages. It began when Baltimore starter Dave McNally walked the bases loaded with one out. The reliever entered the game, got out of the jam, and wound up going 6 2/3, giving up one hit and striking out 11, including six in a row, both World Series records for a reliever. Who was that pitcher?

35. Double: Certain pitchers become linked to specific hitters after giving up a memorable or historic hit to that batter. Start with the man who served up the pitch that Stan Musial doubled into the gap for his 3,000th hit.

Slight clue: the pitcher, who was born in Poland, had his nationality as another point of commonality with Musial.

36. Double: Which New York Mets lefty gave up Roberto Clemente's 3,000th hit? Clue: the pitcher's career was just starting, and starting off well. He was that season's Rookie of the Year. Clemente's career, of course, was nearly over. Contrary to a widely held belief, the game in which he gathered his 3,000th hit was not his last game.

37. Home Run: Sticking with the Pirates of 1972, their season ended in Game Five of the NLCS, and it ended in an unusual way, a walk-off wild pitch. Who uncorked that pitch?

38. Double: On June 29, 1990, baseball history was made when, for the first time ever, two pitchers each threw a no-hitter, just a matter of hours apart and in different cities. Clues: one threw his for the Dodgers, while the other pitcher, who had once been a teammate of the Dodgers pitcher, recorded his no-hitter for the Oakland Athletics. The Los Angeles pitcher was the NL Rookie of the Year as well as the Cy Young Award winner in 1981. The Oakland hurler won 20 games four years in a row (1987–1990) and finished in the top four in Cy Young voting each of those seasons. Name either man.

39. Home Run: The next several questions all relate to pitchers who surrendered famous home runs starting with the man who gave up Babe Ruth's record-setting 60th home run in 1927. Clue: his initials are T.Z.

40. Home Run: Here's another case of take a (blind?) hack at this question because the pitcher who is the answer here is pretty obscure. Who gave up the home run to Babe Ruth in the 1932 World Series which has been labeled Ruth's Called Shot?

41. Home Run: Here's your really long shot at hitting back-to-back-to-back homers. Which pitcher served up the 61st home run to Roger Maris in 1961, allowing him to ease by Ruth's single-season home-run mark?

42. Single: Ozzie Smith hit a memorable home run, too. During the fifth game of the 1985 NLCS, the switch-hitting Smith came to the plate in the majors having gone 3,009 times batting lefty. Over that span he had never hit a homer. Smith's power while hitting righty wasn't exactly impressive, either—he owned 13 career home runs over his eight years in the majors. However, he snapped his left-handed hitting home-run drought, to give his Cardinals a 3–2 win over the Dodgers. Who was on the hill when Smith hit the ball over the right-field wall at Busch Stadium that day? a. Tom Niedenfuer b. Rick Honeycutt c. Alejandro Pena

43. Single: Name the Reds pitcher who gave up Hank Aaron's 714th home run, which tied him with Babe Ruth on the all-time homer list. That shot came on Opening Day of 1974. a. Don Gullett b. Jack Billingham c. Clay Kirby

44. Single: Four days after Aaron's record-tying shot, he came through again to shoot by Ruth. Which Dodger threw the pitch that Aaron deposited over the left-field fence for no. 715? a. Al Downing b. Mike Marshall c. Charlie Hough

45. Double: In 1973, a very good Pittsburgh Pirates pitcher suddenly lost all semblance of control of his pitches. The year before, this man, who owned 100 big-league wins by that season's end, came in second in Cy Young Award voting, winning 19 games and registering a 2.49 ERA. Suddenly, in '73, he simply could not throw strikes—he only walked as many batters as he had the season before (84), but his strikeouts plummeted from 117 to 27, and he led the league in hit batters. Plus, his 84 walks came over a span of just 88 2/3 innings pitched in 1973. Alarmingly, his ERA shot up to an ungodly 9.85 with his winning percentage sinking from .704 in '72 to .250 based on his 3–9 record. The next year he worked five innings in just one game and that outing ended his big-league career. Name this man.

46. Triple: Another pitcher suddenly and inexplicably lost his ability to throw the way he once had, throwing the ball wildly—extremely wildly, to the point where some of his pitches hit the dirt in front of the plate and others sailed to the net behind the plate.

Making this worse was the fact that his issues first manifested themselves during the 2000 postseason with the eyes of the nation upon him. In the NLDS, he retired eight men but walked six and let fly five wild pitches. In the next round, he pitched in two games, walking five and firing four more wild pitches. His playoff ERA stood at 15.75, way up from his regular-season ERA of 3.50. Name this former pitcher who mainly was with the Cardinals.

47. Single: In 2018, a Yankees pitcher's contract was to reward him with a $500,000 performance bonus if he worked 155 innings or more. He entered his last start of the season a handful of innings short of his goal. When he was two innings away from earning his bonus, he apparently hit a batter on purpose, knowing that his actions would lead to him earning an ejection. It also earned him the respect of teammates who realized he was standing up for them after a Tampa Bay pitcher had plunked a Yankee. Given the circumstances, New York decided to pay him the bonus anyway. Who is this man who ended his career with 251 wins?

48. Single: Name the NL East pitcher who set a record at the start of the 2021 season when he recorded 50 strikeouts over his first four starts, breaking a record shared by Nolan Ryan and Shane Bieber with 48 K's.

49. Double: The pitcher from the previous question also tied a record by fanning 14 or more batters in three straight appearances early in 2021. Name either of the two men who had also achieved that feat. Clue: one is a Hall of Famer most famous for his days with the Red Sox and the other pitched for the Pirates, Astros, and was still active in 2021 with the Yankees.

50. Single: Several pitchers have worn rather strange

numbers on their backs. Which reliever, also known as Wild Thing, wore no. 99 at times?

51. Home Run: Like the pitcher from the previous question, this man wore several different jersey numbers, but in 1993 as a Cardinal and in 1995 when he was with the Phillies, he wore "00" because double zeroes resembled his initials, O.O. Name him.

52. Double: Time for another math lesson. Add the jersey number of Clayton Kershaw (every season, starting in the middle of his rookie season) to the number worn by another Dodgers legend, Sandy Koufax. What is the sum of those two numbers?

53. Triple: Subtract the number of Jacob deGrom's uniform from that of Adam Wainwright.

54. Double: Over his long and illustrious career, strikeout king Nolan Ryan wore two different jersey numbers. Add them together.

55. Double: Two Angels pitchers led the AL in strikeouts every season from 1972 through 1979. Name these pitchers.

56. Single: Who set the all-time single-season record for strikeouts when he set down 383 batters on strikes?

57. Single: Who held the season strikeout record with 382 prior to the man who barely broke his mark?

58. Double: Who was the first pitcher to complete a season with a strikeouts per nine innings ratio of nine or better? Clues: he struck out 9.7 batters for every nine innings pitched as a rookie in 1955. His future looked fantastic until he was struck in the eye by a wicked line drive off the bat of Gil McDougald in 1957.

59. Double: A long chain of pitchers would later top the pitcher in question above. It started with Sandy Koufax and his new record of 10.13 and 10.55 K's per nine innings in 1960 and 1962. Who was the man who exceeded Koufax's record in 1965? Clue: he was an AL pitcher (from the same team as the hurler from the previous question) whose nickname related to his speed.

60. Double: More record smashers followed. Dwight Gooden hoisted the record K/9 IP ratio to 11.40 in 1984. Like the pitcher from question 58, Gooden was a rookie when he set the record. Next came Nolan Ryan at 11.48 in 1987, followed by Randy Johnson, the first man to have a ratio of better than 12 strikeouts for every nine innings pitched (12.35 in 1995). Who, in 1998, came next? Clues: amazingly, this man also claimed the record as a rookie. He was, in fact, the NL Rookie of the Year. He gained more fame for what he did in one game than for his ratio record.

61. Single: Not counting Shane Bieber's 14.20 strikeout ratio in the shortened 2020 season, which is the highest ever, name any man between the pitcher mentioned in the last question and Bieber, who held the best single-season ratio of K's per every nine innings.

62. Single: The Arizona Diamondbacks won the 2001 World Series over the Yankees in seven games. All four of the D-backs wins came from two pitchers who worked 38 2/3 of the 65 total innings pitched for the Arizona staff in the Series. Name the two key pitchers who put New York away.

63. Double: In the very first World Series ever held (1903), a Pittsburgh Pirates pitcher named Deacon Phillippe became the first man to win three games in a Series. Of course, that World Series was under the best-of-nine format. More than half a century later, another Pirate was on his way to winning three games in the 1960 World Series when his bullpen allowed the Yankees to take the lead, depriving him of that third victory opportunity. By an uncanny coincidence, the Pittsburgh starter was, like Phillippe, nicknamed Deacon. Name this Cy Young Award winner who nearly made history.

64. Double: Name the pitcher who was the first to win three games in a World Series under the now-standard best-of-seven setup. He went on to be one of the very first inductees into the Hall of Fame.

65. Double: One player broke into the majors by pitching briefly for the Yankees in 1950. Seven seasons later, he won three games against the Yankees in the World Series for the Milwaukee Braves to become the third man named as the Series MVP. Name him.

66. Single: Through 2020, 13 men have won three games in a given World Series, and eight of those pitchers did so over just the first 17 Series played. An explosion of men who won three Series games took place in the 1960s. One of those pitchers is mentioned above, but your job is to name the next one to accomplish this. Clue: he did it in 1967.

67. Double: Which Detroit Tigers pitcher was the next pitcher to turn the three World Series win trick, doing this in 1968? No other pitcher would win three in the Series until Randy Johnson in 2001. The Tigers pitcher secured his third win on two days' rest.

68. Double: Which pitcher set a record by winning seven straight fall classic games over a period of three World Series (1964, 1967, and 1968)? In 1968, he also set a record by striking out 17 in a Series contest.

69. Triple: Winning three games in a World Series is great, but a Yankees reliever once experienced the agony of Series defeat three times. In 1981, he faced the Los Angeles Dodgers in three contests. He retired 11 batters but gave up nine hits and seven runs, all earned. His WHIP was an atrocious 3.273, yet he was coming off a season in which he posted an ERA of 1.63. Name this righty whose initials are G.F.

70. Home Run: Who was the first man to win the MVP Award for the World Series? Clues: this took place in 1955 and the man in question was a 22-year-old (turned 23 during the World Series) Brooklyn Dodger southpaw pitcher who had gone 9–10 on the regular season.

71. Double: Which Florida Marlins pitcher was the MVP of the 2003 World Series?

72. Double: Which Philadelphia Phillies pitcher took home the MVP hardware for his work in the 2008 World Series?

73. Single: Which pitcher, through stats of 2020, holds the lowest ERA ever for World Series play?

74. Single: Name any of the other pitchers in the top five for lowest World Series ERAs of all time.

75. Single: Name any of the pitchers who hold down the numbers six through 10 slots on the list of best World Series ERAs ever.

76. Double: Who was the youngest player to ever appear in a big-league contest? Clues: this "old lefthander" was only pitching because his debut came during World War II when talent was thin due to so many bona fide players serving the country. When he retired from the game, he became a popular baseball broadcaster.

77. Triple: Tricky question—what man became the first player to hit a home run in a World Series game despite never having hit one in the regular season? Clue: this took place in the 1968 Series.

78. Triple: Among pitchers who never threw a no-hitter, who had the most career wins, well over 300?

79. Single: Everyone knows Cy Young owns the most lifetime wins, 511, but can you name any of the next three modern-era pitchers who trail Young?

80. Single: The next pitcher on the list is the winningest lefty ever. Who is this man?

81. Single: Among modern-era pitchers, this is the only man to challenge the pitcher referred to above for lifetime wins by a lefty, but even this all-time great fell 34 wins shy of the lefty wins leader.

82. Double: In 2021, a Baltimore Orioles pitcher threw a no-hitter. Only one man reached base after he struck out but stayed alive when strike three eluded the catcher. Shortly after, the runner was erased on a caught stealing. This game marked the first time a no-hitter missed out on perfect game status due to a wild pitch—normally, this occurs due to an error, walk, or a hit batter. Name the nearly perfect lefty.

83. Single: Through 2020, the last man to throw a perfect game did so in 2012. Name this pitcher who has a regal nickname.

84. Double: What pitcher was given the nickname The Dark Knight of Gotham?

85. Single: Due to a resemblance to a television character, this Detroit Tigers pitcher was called The Bird. Name him.

86. Single: Which dominant Yankees pitcher became known as the Chairman of the Board back in the 1950s and 1960s?

87. Single: Which future Hall of Famer became just the 14th pitcher to give up four homers in an inning in 1994? a. John Smoltz b. Tom Glavine c. Randy Johnson

88. Triple: In 2021, which pitcher set a record by striking out eight or more batters over a span of 20 straight starts?

89. Double: Which Cleveland Indians pitcher started two games less than a month apart in which the opposing starter threw a no-hitter in 2021? His uncle spent 18 seasons in the majors and later became an analyst for the MLB Network.

90. Single: Through 2021, five pitchers have thrown two no-hitters in the same regular season. Name two of them. If you can identify three or more, take credit for a double.

91. Double: Who, in 2016, became the oldest big-leaguer to come up with the first homer of his career? Clues: this pitcher, just three weeks short of his 43rd birthday, hit a 365-foot homer for the Mets.

92. Home Run: Who was the first pitcher to be officially recorded as a loser in a nine-inning no-hitter he had thrown? Clue: he did this in 1964 while with the Houston Colt .45s, losing 1–0 to the Reds.

93. Double: What man won the Rolaids Fireman of the Year Award five times over a six-year period (1980–1985)?

94. Double: What reliever was the 2011 Rookie of the Year with the Braves when he led the league with 46 saves? He also led the NL the next three years in that department with 42, 50, and 47 saves. He was an All-Star with Atlanta, Boston, and the Chicago Cubs.

95. Single: Through 2020, only two active pitchers in that season had 200 or more lifetime wins. Both were on the same 2021 pitching staff. Name either man for your single, or both for a double.

96. Triple: Who is the only knuckleball specialist to win a Cy Young Award?

97. Single: Who is the last man to win 300+ games?

98. Triple: A *Baseball Digest* article pointed out that of the last 10 men to win 300 games, only one notched no. 300 "for the team he represents in Cooperstown." As of the writing of that article, 300-game-winner Roger Clemens was not in the Hall. Who is the pitcher the story was referring to?

99. Single: As mentioned in Chapter One, pitching dominated the 1968 season. Seven pitchers put up ERAs below 2.00. Name two for a single, or three for a two-base hit.

100. Double: Which Dodgers pitcher set a new record in 1968 by firing 58 2/3 successive innings of shutout ball?

101. Single: What pitcher, also a Dodger, broke the record from the previous question, and still holds the record that he established in 1988?

102. Double: Only two men have ever won the Rookie of the Year, the Cy Young, and the MVP Award during their careers. Name one.

103. Single: In addition to the men alluded to above, nine other pitchers won at least one Cy Young Award and an MVP trophy. Name three for a single. Four or more earns a double.

104. Double: Who holds the record for the most appearances in a season, 106?

105. Double: Behind the ironman who worked in 106 games, which two NL pitchers share second place in this department?

CHAPTER TWO ANSWERS: PITCHERS

1. Ralph Terry

2. Hendley was stingy that night, giving up just one hit, two base runners, and one unearned run, but that was enough to do him in. Hendley carried a no-hitter into the seventh inning. The win for Koufax represented his fourth and final no-hitter. The Dodger great fanned 14 batters, which set a record for the most strikeouts ever in a perfect game (tied by Matt Cain in 2012). Hendley and Koufax also established a record for the fewest total base runners, two, in a perfect game. By way of contrast to today's games, the perfecto lasted a mere 1 hour and 43 minutes.

3. Eric Show

4. Justin Verlander

5. Aroldis Chapman. Lighting up the radar gun at 100+ mph was mere routine for him.

6. Tim Stoddard. He won the basketball title in March of 1974, and earned his World Series ring in 1983.

7. Shane Bieber

8. Dennis Martinez. He held the record for the most wins by a Nicaraguan, and he was the first man from that country to play in the majors.

9. Sam McDowell. He whiffed 300+ twice. Koufax did that three times.

10. Pedro Martinez. In 2000, his ERA of 1.74 was 3.17 earned runs lower than the AL ERA. He also owns the second best ERA gap in AL history.

11. Greg Maddux. His 1.56 ERA in 1994 was 2.65 earned runs better than the NL mark. Like Martinez, Maddux also has the second best ERA difference in his league.

12. Dallas Keuchel. In 2016, his win total fell by 11 to 9 wins and his ERA ballooned more than two runs to 4.55.

13. Dallas Braden. His career record is 26–36.

14. Bob Ojeda survived the wreck—the other two men were Steve Olin and Tim Crews.

15. José Fernández

16. True

17. Antonio Alfonseca

18. Mordecai "Three Fingers" Brown

19. Justin Verlander in 2011 when he was with the Tigers.

20. Dodgers pitcher Clayton Kershaw won the NL MVP Award in 2014.

21. Trevor Bauer. He had a reported salary of $40 million in 2021.

22. Vida Blue. He was the AL starter in the 1971 and

1975 All-Star Games as an Oakland Athletic, and the starting pitcher for the NL in the mid-summer classic of 1978 when he was with the Giants.

23. Stone, who went on to become a broadcaster, finished his career with the Baltimore Orioles.

24. Gooden kicked around towards the end of his career, bouncing from his original club, the Mets, to the Yankees, the Indians, then to two teams most fans forget he was with, the Astros and Devil Rays. His final season, 2000, was split between Houston, Tampa Bay, and, the answer to this question, the Yankees.

25. Wagner ended up with Atlanta and, at the age of 38, did quite well. He went 7–2 with 37 saves and an ERA of 1.43 to conclude his career with 422 saves (although he never once led his league in that category).

26. The Detroit Tigers. In his first year with the Yankees, Miller had 36 saves after having recorded only two for his nine seasons up to that point. However, he then joined Cleveland where he earned only seven saves in three years, yet his impact there was huge. Francona would bring him into a game in virtually any late inning when there was a strong, imminent threat such as the heart of an opponent's lineup due at the plate. Saves mainly went to closer Cody Allen, but Miller was vital to the team and in 2016 they made it to the World Series for the first time since 1954.

27. Schilling began his big-league days with the Orioles, but it was not an auspicious beginning. He went 0–3 with a sky high 9.82 ERA, giving no indication that he'd go on to win nearly 60 percent of his decisions (.597) and endure for 20 seasons.

28. All-Star Jerry Reuss began his playing days with the St. Louis Cardinals.

29. Fingers won numerous awards including a Cy Young Award and the MVP Award in 1981 when he helped the Brewers earn a postseason spot while sporting an ERA of 1.04. After spending many years with the Oakland Athletics and the Padres, he did, in fact, end his career with Milwaukee.

30. Matlack was released by the Texas Rangers after the 1983 season, ending his years in the majors. As good as he was (3.18 lifetime ERA, 30 shutouts, 1,500+ strike-outs), he had a losing record for his career at 125–126.

31. McLain moved on from Washington to Oakland then to Atlanta, where his up and down 10-year career came to a screeching halt when he was released prior to the 1973 season. As a side note, for his glowing production in 1968 he earned a paltry $33,000 (but after that showing he did get a boost that nearly doubled his salary, up to $65,000). His peak salary was a reported $90,000.

32. Johnny Sain. He was a 24-game winner in 1948, his third 20-win season in a row. Warren Spahn, the other stud, won 15 in 1948, giving the Braves 39 of their 91 wins. Therefore, Boston fans who sang out the "pray for rain" chant seemingly wished Spahn and Sain would pitch back-to-back games, then they hoped rain would wash out enough games until those two could come back, start, and hopefully, win two more games. The team's other three primary starters went a combined 31–26.

Sain went on to become one of the most highly touted, famous pitching coaches ever, spending 17 years coaching. Under his tutelage 16 20-game winners emerged, including some who came out of nowhere. The list includes Whitey Ford, Al Downing, Jim Perry, Jim Bouton, Ralph Terry, Mudcat Grant, Denny McLain (who won 31 under Sain in 1968 after going 17–16 the year before), Earl Wilson (who had his only 20-win season under Sain), Stan Bahnsen, Jim Kaat, and Wilbur Wood. Sain was on the staff of six clubs and, in the 1960s, five of his teams won pennants.

33. Frank Tanana. He and Nolan Ryan inspired the phrase that alluded to the fact that the two stars could win big, but they'd be followed in the rotation by several not-so-stellar hurlers. Many of the California Angels seasons in the 1970s were poor despite Tanana who, in 1974, had a 3.12 ERA yet lost 19 games for a cellar-dwelling team. That same season, Ryan was responsible for 22 of his team's 68 victories, but he was one of only two pitchers with 13 or more innings pitched to finish with a record above .500—Bill Singer went 7–4.

34. Moe Drabowsky

35. Moe Drabowsky again. Musial's hit came against the Cubs on May 13, 1958, when he became the first man to collect his 3,000th hit as a pinch-hitter. The Cardinals wanted Musial to reach his milestone back home in St. Louis, so they didn't start him that day. However, the game situation eventually called for Musial to come off the bench and he came through with his hit.

Drabowsky, who had a great sense of humor and pulled many tricks, called himself the Polish Prince of Pranks.

36. Jon Matlack surrendered a double to Clemente for his historic hit. That hit was his last regular-season hit, and it did come in his last at bat in regular-season play (in the fourth inning; Bill Mazeroski pinch-hit for Clemente the following inning). However, Clemente played again three days later in the Pirates' next game, their second to last game. In that contest, he came off the bench to play right field for the ninth inning. Further, Clemente played again in the 1972 National League Championship Series. Therefore, his very last hit (a first-inning single) and his final plate appearance (an intentional walk) came on October 11, 1972.

37. Bob Moose. Johnny Bench had led off the ninth inning with a game-tying solo home run. Two singles and a fly ball that moved pinch-runner George Foster to third set the stage for Moose's wild pitch.

38. The L.A. pitcher was Fernando Valenzuela. The Oakland star was Dave Stewart.

39. Tom Zachary gave up Ruth's 60th homer in 1927.

40. Charlie Root. If you got the right answer for this question or the previous one, take a bow. Root was not an obscure name during his playing days—he led the NL in wins in 1927 with 26 and, with 201 lifetime victories, he remains the winningest pitcher in Cubs history. His Cubs made it to four World Series, coincidentally in every third year from 1929 through 1938. Since that fourth World Series in '38, through 2020 the Cubs have managed to make it back to the fall classic just twice, losing it in 1945 then finally winning it all in 2016.

A film of the Called Shot discovered in 1999 seems to prove that Ruth did not point to the center-field bleachers in order to call his shot, but the legend persists. Many experts feel Ruth did point, but angrily, and to the Cubs dugout, not the outfield, as he was jawing with Chicago players.

41. Tracy Stallard was the victim of Maris's 61st home run.

42. a. Niedenfuer. Smith's shocking blow led Cards broadcaster Jack Buck to shout out his now famous line, "Go crazy, folks! Go crazy!"

43. b. Jack Billingham. Aaron wasted no time tying Ruth, propelling the historic home run in the first inning of the first game of the 1974 season. After Ralph Garr drew a walk, Mike Lum singled, and Darrell Evans flew out, Aaron followed with his home run.

44. a. Al Downing. Once more, Aaron wasted little time before homering. He drew a walk leading off the second inning, but in the fourth with Darrell Evans on board, Aaron lifted a Downing pitch over the left-field fence for his 715th lifetime home run.

45. Steve Blass. People compared his wildness to a golfer suffering from a case of the "yips." He did, however, go on to have a splendid career as a very popular Pirates broadcaster.

46. Rick Ankiel. His pitching days were over in 2004, but he decided to try his hand at playing the outfield, knowing he had been a pretty good hitting pitcher. He wound up lasting through 2013, leaving the game as a .240 hitter who hit a personal high of 25 homers in 2008.

47. CC Sabathia

48. Jacob deGrom. Bieber had tied Ryan's record the weekend before deGrom usurped him.

49. Pedro Martinez in 1999 and Gerrit Cole in 2019

50. Mitch Williams

51. Omar Olivares

52. Kershaw wore no. 22. Add that to the no. 32 worn by Koufax to come up with the answer of 54.

53. Wainwright's primary jersey number was 50 (he

wore no. 60 as a rookie), and deGrom's number is 48. Therefore, the answer here is 2.

54. Ryan wore no. 34 for the majority of his 27 years in the majors, but he also wore no. 30 in 12 of his seasons. The answer for this question is 64.

55. Nolan Ryan and Frank Tanana. Of course, Ryan was responsible for seven of those eight seasons, missing out only in 1975 when Tanana blew it by 269 batters. That year Ryan only made 28 starts.

56. Nolan Ryan. Not only did he fan 383 batters in 1973, but over the span mentioned in the last question, Ryan topped the 300-strikeout level five times over eight years.

57. Sandy Koufax. His single-season high of 382 K's came in 1965 in his next to last season at the age of 29. Ryan entered his last start of the 1973 season 15 strikeouts shy of the Koufax record. At the end of the ninth inning, he had tied the mark. Luckily for him, the game was also tied. It took Ryan until the 11th inning to break the record when he struck out Rich Reese. It turned out Reese was the last batter he faced that season, as Ryan's Angels, with just a few games remaining on the schedule, won the game in the last half of the 11th, giving Ryan his 21st win of the season in front of a crowd of just 9,100.

58. Herb Score. He led the AL in strikeouts in both his rookie and sophomore seasons with 245 and 263

K's. The next year, the year of his injury, he saw action in just five games, and he would never again strike out more than 147 men. His career was over in 1962 when he worked relief in just four contests.

59. Cleveland's Sudden Sam McDowell. His record ratio was 10.71.

60. Kerry Wood with a 12.58 ratio which, naturally, didn't get the headlines his 20-strikeout performance got that season. In just his fifth big-league start, Wood dominated the Houston Astros, allowing just a third-inning single on a line drive which nearly was snagged (it glanced off the top of Kevin Orie's glove at third base). Wood also hit Craig Biggio with a pitch in the sixth inning, but that was it.

61. After Wood, Pedro Martinez held the record for two years. Next came Randy Johnson at 13.41 from 2001 until Gerrit Cole had a 13.82 ratio in 2019.

62. Curt Schilling won one game (1.69 ERA) and Randy Johnson won three (1.04 ERA). The two men were named co-MVPs for the World Series. Johnson not only won Game Six to keep Arizona alive, he came back on no rest the next day to get the final win. Against him, the Yankees' sad story that day was one of four men up, and four men down.

63. Vern Law

64. Christy Mathewson. He was utterly superb in the

1905 World Series. He started three games, turned in three complete games, and won each contest via shutouts. Always possessing pinpoint control, he walked one batter vs. 18 strikeouts, and surrendered just 13 hits for a WHIP of 0.519. In addition, Mathewson's three wins came over a period of six days.

By the way, thanks in part to the games taking place during the age of the dead ball, each of the five games resulted in shutouts. The Giants' pitching was almost flawless—their team ERA was 0.00 as they gave up a total of just three runs to the Philadelphia Athletics. The Giants gave up a mere five walks and 24 hits over 45 innings of sheer superiority.

65. Lew Burdette. He fired two shutouts and had an ERA of 0.67 vs. New York in the Series. He blanked the Yanks over his last 24 innings pitched in the Series. His real first name is Selva, which isn't too far off the spelling of the word "saliva." That's quite fitting for a man accused of throwing the spitball.

66. Bob Gibson

67. Mickey Lolich. Although it was Denny McLain, who won 31 games in 1968, and not Lolich who was the ace of the Tigers staff, Lolich was brilliant in the Series, defeating Gibson and his Cardinals while McLain went 1–2 with an ERA almost twice that of Lolich's 1.67.

68. Bob Gibson. His seven-game winning streak in World Series play was broken by Lolich in Game Seven of the 1968 Series. Nevertheless, in that Series Gibson struck out 35 Tigers and walked only four while putting up a glistening 1.67 ERA—his lifetime ERA in Series play was 1.89.

69. George Frazier

70. Johnny Podres

71. Josh Beckett. Even though he was only 1–1 against the Yankees, he helped the Marlins win the World Championship, nailing down the Series-winning game with a shutout. He was miserly on the mound, giving up just two earned runs over 16 1/3 innings and putting up a WHIP of .0796.

72. Cole Hamels. In the previous round of the postseason he had also been named the MVP, lifting his Phils over the Dodgers in the NLCS. In the World Series, he won the opener vs. Tampa Bay and was instrumental in the Phillies' final win in Game Five as well.

73. Madison Bumgarner. Among pitchers with 20 or more innings of World Series work, his ERA of 0.25 stands supreme. He went 4–0 over five games and 36 lifetime innings pitched, and he can brag of a 0.528 WHIP. Few fans will forget what he did in the 2014 Series vs. the Kansas City Royals: he went seven innings in Game One and the distance in Game Five, winning 7–1 and 5–0; then, three days after his shutout, he toiled five innings out of the bullpen to cement his Giants 3–2 win to earn a save and wrap things up in Game Seven. The Series MVP was responsible for just the third save (regular season or otherwise) of five innings or more over the previous 25 seasons.

74. The second best career World Series ERA belongs to Jack Billingham (0.36). He is followed by Harry "The Cat" Brecheen at 0.83, Claude Osteen (0.86), and Babe Ruth (0.87).

75. The sixth through tenth best Series ERAs have been turned in by Sherry Smith (0.89), Sandy Koufax (0.95), Christy Mathewson (0.97), Mariano Rivera (0.99), and Hippo Vaughn (1.00).

76. Joe Nuxhall of the Cincinnati Reds, who wasn't even 16 when he broke into the Bigs. He was a mere 15 years and 316 days old when he made his June 10, 1944, debut. The St. Louis Cardinals shellacked him. He lasted 2/3 of an inning in a 18–0 drubbing. His pitching line was ugly: five runs on five walks and two hits with a wild pitch thrown in. He would not work again in the majors until 1952, and he took off from there, winning 135 games and lasting 15 seasons.

77. Mickey Lolich

78. Grover Cleveland Alexander

79. Walter Johnson (417), then Grover Alexander and Mathewson (tied with 373)

80. Warren Spahn, with 363 wins

81. Steve Carlton. He won 329 games. Based on the way today's game is played, the men mentioned above should hold on to their elite spots for a long, long time (forever?).

82. John Means. Before his gem, he had never gone beyond seven innings in the majors.

83. Felix Hernandez, a.k.a. King Felix, of the Mariners

84. Matt Harvey

85. Mark Fidrych

86. Whitey Ford. He had a .690 winning percentage over 16 seasons. When Ford retired, only one modern-era pitcher had a better percentage, Spud Chandler at .717, who benefited from playing with the Yankees from 1937 through 1947. Chandler's best season's winning percentage was .833.

87. a. Smoltz. He also gave up 20 total bases that inning, the most in NL play since 1900.

88. Cleveland's Shane Bieber

89. Zach Plesac. He took the loss against White Sox no-hit pitcher Carlos Rodon and wound up with a no-decision when Cincinnati's Wade Miley threw his no-hitter. Zach's uncle is Dan Plesac.

90. Johnny Vander Meer threw no-hitters in

back-to-back starts in 1938. In 1951, Allie Reynolds threw two no-hitters and Virgil Trucks matched him the following season. Next came Nolan Ryan in 1973. Most recently, Max Scherzer turned the trick in 2015.

91. Bartolo Colon. A rookie in 1997, Colon would not clear the fences until nearly his final season (he retired in 2018). Interestingly, the 2016 season not only featured his first and only homer, but the first and only time he drew a walk as well.

92. Ken Johnson. In the top of the ninth, Pete Rose rambled all the way to second base on a throwing error by Johnson. He advanced on a groundout and scored when Vada Pinson also reached via an error. You're a whiz if you got this one correct!

93. Dan Quisenberry. From 1980 through 1985, he also led the AL in saves five times.

94. Craig Kimbrel

95. Justin Verlander and Zack Greinke

96. R.A. Dickey. Trivia note: Dickey was born without an ulnar collateral ligament, UCL, in his pitching elbow. That meant he would never require Tommy John surgery for a torn UCL.

97. Randy Johnson in 2009—did you recall he won no. 300 with the Giants? He went on to win three more games. Many experts believe that with the way the game is played today, with starters getting fewer starts, innings, and decisions than they once did, there may never again be a 300-game winner.

98. Steve Carlton. He won his 300th game with the Phillies then tacked on an additional handful of wins with four other clubs.

99. Bob Gibson and Bob Bolin in the NL and Luis Tiant, Sam McDowell, Dave McNally, Denny McLain, and Tommy John in the AL Additionally, six other pitchers had ERAs of 2.20 or lower.

Gibson had a 1.12 ERA and a record of 22–9. Something Yogi Berra observed about a 25–5 season by Sandy Koufax would certainly also apply to Gibson's record in '68: "I can see how he won 25 games. What I don't understand is how he lost five." How true: just how *did* Gibson lose nine in '68?

100. Don Drysdale, in his next to last season. Somehow he only went 14–12 on the season, even with a 2.15 ERA.

101. Orel Hershiser. He threw 59 consecutive shutout innings to end the 1988 season. In his first start of 1989, he surrendered a run in the very first inning. Although it didn't count towards his record, he began the 1988 postseason with eight more shutout innings, giving him 67 in a row that season.

102. Don Newcombe won the 1949 Rookie of the Year honors and he was the Cy Young Award winner as well as the NL MVP in 1956. Justin Verlander was the AL Rookie of the Year in 2006. In 2011, he won the MVP; and he copped the Cy Young Award in 2011 and 2019.

103. Clayton Kershaw, Rollie Fingers, Dennis Eckersley, Willie Hernandez, Roger Clemens, Sandy Koufax, Vida Blue, Bob Gibson, and Denny McLain.

104. Mike Marshall when he was with the Dodgers. He also holds the AL record for the most games pitched in a season with 90.

105. Kent Tekulve (in 1979) and Salomon Torres (in 2006). Both worked in 94 games with the Pittsburgh Pirates.

CHAPTER THREE
MANAGERS AND TEAMS

1. Double: Which team became the first one ever to have three of its players hit 40+ homers in a season? Score this one a homer if you can name those players.

2. Single: Which Tampa Bay manager received strong criticism for a move he made in the 2020 World Series when he elected to replace his starter, the Cy Young Award–winning Blake Snell, even though the next men due up in the Los Angeles batting order had gone a collective 0-for-6 with six strikeouts against his ace? Snell was winning 1–0 on a two-hitter, had thrown just 73 pitches, and the game was only in the sixth inning. The move backfired and the Dodger won the Series that night.

3. Triple: When Shane Bieber won the 2020 Cy Young Award, he became the fifth Cleveland Indian to capture that honor. Name three of the other four men to accomplish this.

4. Single: In 2021, this manager, already a Hall of Famer, returned to the majors after nine years being out of a managerial job.

5. Single: In 2021, another man returned to the managing ranks after a one-year ban was imposed on him for his 2017 involvement in Houston's sign-stealing scandal. Name him.

6. Single: Another man obtained a managerial job in 2021 after being suspended for one year. He was the Astros bench coach in 2017, then moved on to manage Boston before he was hit with his punishment for his role in the sign-stealing affair.

7. Triple: Although this man is much more famous for his groundbreaking ways as a general manager than for what he did as a manager or player, he did set a record once as a catcher. During a 1907 game he allowed 13 stolen bases and threw out nobody. Who is this man?

8. Single: In 2001, which AL team tied the all-time record for wins (116) in a season?

9. Home Run: Which NL team had established that record in 1906?

10. Single: Name the man who played his final big-league game with the Cubs, then, and with no major-league managerial experience, was hired as their manager in 2020.

11. Single: Which manager has guided the Padres and Giants and won three World Series starting with the 2010 title, winning it all every other year over five seasons?

12. Double: Name either of the two teams that joined the majors when it expanded in 1998.

13. Single: In the modern era, only two clubs have switched leagues—name either.

14. Single: Name two of the big-league teams Pete Rose played for. Name all three for a double.

15. Single: Which Arizona Diamondback got the Game Seven hit vs. Mariano Rivera to give the D-backs the World Series in 2001?

16. Single: True or false—the man mentioned in the previous question became the first player that the Diamondbacks honored by retiring his jersey number.

17. Double: Name two of the four future Hall of Famers who were members of the 1997 Orioles.

18. Double: Through 2020, which AL team has produced more Rookies of the Year than any other club in their league?

19. Double: The Dodgers are tops overall in this realm with twice as many winners of that rookie award than the AL leader (again, through 2020). Often when the Dodgers won that award they did so in streaks. From 1947 through 1953, Brooklyn had four players named as the top rookie—name two.

20. Double: A Dodger won the award 30 percent of

the time in the 1960s. Name one of the three Dodgers involved.

21. Single: The next impressive stretch came from 1979 through 1982 when a Dodger was selected as the Rookie of the Year in each of those seasons. Name either the second baseman or one of the three pitchers to cop that award.

22. Single: As impressive as the above streak was, from 1992 through 1996, a Dodger took home that award in *five* consecutive seasons. Name one of these players.

23. Single: The Dodgers appeared in the World Series more than any other NL club, 21 times. However, which NL franchise has *won* the most World Series (11)?

24. Double: Which ballpark was the site of Hank Aaron's record-setting 715th home run?

25. Double: What was the name of the Astros home ballpark from 2000 to 2002 until a scandal hit, one that rocked the company for which the park had been named?

26. Single: In June of 2002, the Astros re-named their home field Minute Maid Park, but they aren't the only club to play in a park named after an orange juice/beverage company—name the other one.

27. Single: Which ballpark is recognized as the one

which ushered in the era of the neoclassical parks or the retro ballparks?

28. Single: What was the name of the Reds' home ballpark for the majority of the time from 1912 through part of the 1970 season?

29. Single: For many decades ballparks didn't take the names of corporations such as Progressive Field or Comerica Park. It was more normal to have names such as Milwaukee County Stadium or Forbes Field in Pittsburgh, given that title to honor a British general who came up with the name for the city. Sure, some old parks bore the names of families that ran big businesses such as Wrigley Field, named after the family that owned the chewing gum company. However, most parks' names were not tied in with corporations. Today the situation is the opposite. Your question: which current NL team plays in a ballpark, which happens to be one of the oldest parks still in use, that's name is not linked to a business?

30. Double: Through 2020, Tampa Bay has retired the number of only one of their players, and that man was with the club quite briefly at that. Who is he?

31. Single: For many, many years there were only 16 teams in Major League Baseball. Then, in 1961 and 1962, four new teams, two in each league, joined the Bigs. Name three of the four teams born in either the AL in '61, or the NL in '62.

32. Single: Of the four teams from the previous question, one set a modern-day record for futility, losing more games than any other major-league team had done to date. Which team is this?

33. Single: Another round of expansion, upping the ranks of the majors to 24 teams, took place in 1969, the first season in which the majors were divided into divisions. Name two of the four new franchises from that season.

34. Double: How many years did the first major-league team located in Seattle stay in that city before it relocated?

35. Single: Which four teams that were charter members of the AL still play in the same city as they were born in way back in 1901?

36. Single: Dating back to the 1800s, four teams had the word "stockings" as part of their nickname for some time. St. Louis was known as the Brown Stockings for one season, and the Cubs were called the White Stockings for a period of time. Two clubs went by Red Stockings—the Braves for seven seasons when they began in Boston, and one other NL team which you have to identify.

37. Double: Only a few teams have had three different cities as their home base. The most obscure team is what we now call the Orioles. In their first season ever, 1901, they were the Milwaukee Brewers before shuffling off to

St. Louis the next year where they became the Browns. In 1954 they moved to Baltimore. Name the other two teams to call three different cities their home.

38. Double: When Houston first began as a big-league franchise, what was its nickname?

39. Single: In 1969, when MLB went to division play, to which division were the Braves assigned? a. NL East b. NL West c. NL Central

40. Single: Only two teams have ever been switched from one league to the other one. Name either team.

41. Double: One NL team for years and years was given the annual honor of hosting the first game of each new season (with a few exceptions). Their Opener became a rich baseball tradition.

42. Single: In the early stages of the 2021 season the only active big-league team that had never recorded a no-hitter finally joined the club. What team is this?

43. Home Run: Related question—the last no-hitter before the one touched on above came in September of 2020 when Alec Mills of the Cubs threw one vs. the Brewers. Coincidentally, both the Cubs' no-hit pitcher and the man mentioned in the last question had the same teammate working behind the plate for them. Name him.

44. Single: In what year did the Amazin' Mets cast

off their loser label and stun the baseball world by winning their first World Series to solidify their name as the Miracle Mets? a. 1966 b. 1969 c. 1973 d. 1986

45. Double: Which season featured the Orioles capturing the World Series over the Reds? That was the year third baseman Brooks Robinson put on a one-man show, coming up with dazzling plays to rob the Reds of sure hits.

46. Double: The St. Louis Cardinals of the Gashouse Gang era won a World Series over the Detroit Tigers in which of the following seasons (below)? First a clue: this was the year the Dean brothers, Dizzy and Daffy, won all four of the Cards' victories. a. 1926 b. 1931 c. 1934

47. Single: The 1966 season featured the Baltimore Orioles winning the World Series in a sweep. Baltimore only hit .200 as a team and managed to score just 3.25 runs per game, but that was enough. The O's pitching staff exhibited sensational stuff, winning the final three games by shutouts, including back-to-back 1–0 victories in Games Three and Four. They even put together a stretch of 33 straight shutout innings for a World Series record. Which team did they put away?

48. Double: As good as the Orioles staff was in the 1966 World Series, one team's staff was even more stingy, defeating the Philadelphia Athletics in five games while posting an inconceivable team ERA of 0.00! This team used just three pitchers, including their biggest stars, Christy Mathewson and Iron Man Joe McGinnity. Name this team, which won 105 games during the regular season.

49. Double: In 2021, a big-league team became just the second team ever to tip off three straight seasons using three different home ballparks. Clue: COVID-19 is a key to this answer.

50. Double: In 2017 an AL team went on a tear, setting a league record with their 22 straight wins. Which club managed this streak?

51. Home Run: As impressive as that streak was, the all-time record is 26 straight wins (with a tie tossed in during that streak). Which team set that record a long, long time ago?

52. Double: Which team had an owner, Charlie Finley, who was a poor man's Bill Veeck, perpetually trying to come up with clever innovations? One was his idea to use an orange baseball, and in a 1973 spring-training game a ball which was dyed orange was, in fact, used in a game (but poorly received). Finley once offered his players a $300 incentive for growing mustaches and many, including Rollie Fingers of handlebar mustache fame, took him up on the offer.

53. Single: One team owner decided to make himself the team's manager. Though Ted Turner's term as his team's skipper lasted only one day, he did run the club back in 1977 before the NL president Chub Feeney (with the backing of baseball commissioner Bowie Kuhn) put a stop to the shenanigans. Which team did Turner manage?

54. Single: Who was the Angels owner who had made his fortune as a musician, songwriter, and actor? He appeared in more than ninety films and was the composer of *Here Comes Santa Claus*.

55. Single: Which team had an owner who was notorious for firing managers at an alarming rate, and for being overly hands-on in the running of the team, seemingly expecting his players to win every game they played. Not winning a World Series in any given year grated on this man. Which team did he own from 1973, when he purchased the team from CBS, until his death in 2010?

56. Double: From 1975 through 1978, what team wore numbers on the front left hip on their uniform pants?

57. Single: Which team was the first one to begin the practice of honoring a player by retiring his uniform number? Clue: they did it in 1939 to honor an ailing legend.

58. Single: On September 27, 1999, Detroit played their final game in Tiger Stadium.

To honor some Detroit legends from the past, the Tigers starters that day wore the same uniform number as had been worn by former greats at their position.

Why did the Tigers send Gabe Kapler to center field with a uniform adorned with no number?

59. Home Run: Which team, said to be copying the use of uniform numbers in hockey and football, was the first team to have their players wear jersey numbers? This took place in the AL beginning on June 26, 1916, but the idea didn't take hold until much later.

60. Single: In May of 2021, a NL team acquired a three-time MVP. That gave them four men who owned at least one MVP Award. Name this blessed-with-talent team.

61. Single: Name two of the four MVP winners on that team. Name three to earn a double for this question.

62. Single: Which owner of a NL team acquired pitcher Andy Messersmith and promptly told him that above his jersey number 17, the word "channel," instead of his last name, would be sewn to the shirt? Clue: this was an advertising gimmick on the part of the team owner who also owned a TV station, channel 17.

63. Double: The next several questions challenge your knowledge of ballpark traditions and quirks. Start with the fans of a team who delight in roaring out one specific word of the National Anthem prior to home games with gusto. When the song gets to the line, "Oh, say does that . . .," the fans can drown out any singer as they punch the "O" sound, and with good reason. Which team has had this long-standing tradition?

64. Single: Which park from long ago featured a super fan named Hilda Chester who, among other things, rang a cowbell, and raucously rooted her team on? It was the same park that featured a 3-feet high and 30-feet long sign on the outfield wall which read, "Hit Sign, Win Suit." If a player managed to hit the advertisement, he was given a suit from local clothing store proprietor Abe Stark.

65. Triple: Hall of Fame broadcaster Ernie Harwell spoke affectionately of an old park that featured "a big scoreboard with a Chesterfield sign" which, like the Schaefer beer sign in Brooklyn, served to show fans how a play was scored. "If it was ruled a hit, the 'H' in Chesterfield lit up, and if it was an error, an 'E' lit up," recalled Harwell. Name that park.

66. Single: A current park gave birth to a tradition of throwing back a baseball if it had been hit into the stands for a home run by an opponent. At times when a fan appeared to be reluctant to part with the souvenir, other fans, employing the tactic known as peer group pressure, would chant, "Throw it back! Throw it back!" In 1969, the faithful fans who sat in the then-cheap out-field seats became known as the Bleacher Bums.

67. Single: Either come up with the famous nickname of the original Yankee Stadium, or, within three years either way, tell what year that park opened.

68. Double: Which NL team once played in a park which was dubbed the Launching Pad?

69. Double: Which AL team set a record by losing 21 straight games to open a season? This occurred in 1988.

70. Single: Who was the colorful man who was the first manager of the New York Mets?

71. Single: Which legend, who spent his entire managerial career of 53 years in charge of two teams housed in Pennsylvania, owns the most career victories?

72. Single: For an eon John McGraw was the second winningest manager ever, but in 2021 someone took over McGraw's slot—name him.

73. Double: Who was the manager of the 1979 "We Are Family" Pittsburgh Pirates?

74. Single: Who managed the 1984 Detroit Tigers, a team that went wire-to-wire in first place? They stormed to a 18–2 record in the season's opening month, went 19–7 in May, then coasted to 104 wins and a World Series title in five games over the San Diego Padres.

75. Double: From 1979 through 2020, only two teams won consecutive World Series. The Yankees did this from 1998 through 2000. The other team, Toronto, accomplished this in 1992 and 1993. Who was their manager back then?

76. Single: Who managed the Giants when they won three World Series titles, doing this in alternating years from 2010 through 2014?

77. Single: Five managers have won three World Championships over a five-year period. One is the man from the previous question. Name three of the managers to achieve this feat for a single, or identify four for a double.

CHAPTER THREE ANSWERS: MANAGERS AND TEAMS

1. The 1973 Atlanta Braves with Hank Aaron (40), Darrell Evans (41), and Davey Johnson (43)

2. Kevin Cash

3. Corey Kluber in 2017 and 2014, Cliff Lee in 2008, CC Sabathia in 2007, and Gaylord Perry back in 1972. Over a 14-year period a Cleveland pitcher won the Cy Young Award in more than one-third of the seasons, five times in all. Cleveland eventually let all four of the men mentioned above depart via trades.

They also traded Trevor Bauer in 2019, and he went on to win the Cy Young Award the next season. In one year his ERA evaporated from 4.48 to a league-leading 1.73 in 2020, and his value went from being like that of a penny stock to sheer blue chip. However, after sexual assault allegations were leveled against him in June of 2021, he was placed on paid administrative leave by his Dodgers. His last appearance in a Dodgers uniform came on June 28, 2021, and experts speculated at the time that he would never again pitch for them.

4. Tony La Russa, returning to the White Sox, the first team he ever managed

5. A.J. Hinch

6. Alex Cora, back with Boston

7. Branch Rickey. Trivia note: his son, Branch Jr., was nicknamed Twig.

8. The Mariners

9. The Cubs, who won their 116 games in a 152-game season, compared to the 162 games the M's played in 2001

10. David Ross

11. Bruce Bochy. Highly respected for his 25-year body of work and his 2,003 wins, surprisingly his career record is 26 games under .500.

12. Arizona and Tampa Bay

13. The Brewers and Astros

14. The Reds, Phillies, and Expos

15. Luis Gonzalez, a man who happens to be the father of triplets

16. True

17. Roberto Alomar, Mike Mussina, Cal Ripken Jr., and Harold Baines

18. The Yankees, with nine winners

19. Jackie Robinson, the first recipient of the honor, then Don Newcombe, Joe Black, and Jim Gilliam

20. Frank Howard, Jim Lefebvre, and Ted Sizemore

21. Rick Sutcliffe, Steve Howe, Fernando Valenzuela, and Steve Sax

22. Eric Karros, Mike Piazza, Raul Mondesi, Hideo Nomo, and Todd Hollandsworth. From 1947 to 2020, 74 NL players won this award and almost exactly 25 percent of those men have been Dodgers. It's no wonder this has been a highly successful franchise for many of their years in existence since '47 (making it to the World Series 18 times).

23. The Cardinals

24. Atlanta Fulton County Stadium

25. Enron Field—the Enron Corporation paid $100 million for the naming rights to the ballpark. Their name was to be used for 30 years, but just two years after signing their agreement, a scandal hit the energy company forcing them to declare bankruptcy, and they sold the rights back to the Astros for $2.1 million. Enron stock once sold at $90.75 per share, but the day they declared bankruptcy, it had plunged to 26 cents per share.

26. The Rays of Tropicana Field

27. Camden Yards—the actual, full name of that venue is Oriole Park at Camden Yards.

28. Crosley Field, but it was also known as Redland Field at times.

29. Los Angeles, which plays in Dodger Stadium. The oldest park still in use, Fenway Park also has no ties to a company's name.

30. Wade Boggs, but the team also retired the number of Don Zimmer as well as, of course, Jackie Robinson, whose number is retired by every big-league club. Boggs spent the final two seasons of his career with Tampa Bay and only 210 of his 3,010 hits came with them.

31. In 1961 the AL expanded by giving franchises to the Los Angeles Angels and a new version of the Washington Senators—the Senators who had been entrenched in Washington D.C. since 1901 (as a charter member of their league) packed up their belongings and moved to Minnesota to become the Twins. The following season the two new teams to join the NL were the Houston Colt .45s (now Astros) and the New York Mets.

32. The Mets. There's an old expression in baseball that states that every team, no matter how bad they are, will win at least one-third of their games, and every team, no matter how good, will lose a third of their games—it's what teams do with the last third that determines what kind of season they'll have. Well, the expansion Mets were so woeful, they were incapable of winning a third of their contests. In fact, they were so horrendous they *almost* didn't win *one-fourth* of their games. They wound up winning exactly one out of every four games they played (.250 WL%), with 40 victories and an abysmal 120 losses.

Hard to believe, but one pre-1900 team from an early Cleveland franchise, a NL team known as the Spiders, were much worse than the Mets. The Spiders anguished through pro baseball's worst season ever. Their 1899 squad, playing in the team's last year of existence, went 20–134 for a "winning" percentage of .130. That meant the pitiful '62 Mets were, mathematically at least, almost twice as good as those Spiders.

The Spiders were 11–101 (no misprint) during away games and lost 40 of their last 41 contests, including 24 in a row over one sad stretch. They only played 42 home games because, understandably, they couldn't draw flies to their ballpark. Reportedly, one game was witnessed by 70 spectators, so they arranged to change their original schedule, taking to the road over and over again.

Overall, though, the franchise wasn't too bad. As a

matter of fact, the season before they could only muster a .130 winning percentage, they posted a winning percentage of .544, winning 61 games more than they would in 1899. Of course, the 1898 team featured Cy Young (25–13) and the 1899 team did not—their primary pitcher, Jim Hughey, started 36 games and went 4–30 in an apparent case of try, try again (and lose, lose again).

33. The AL expanded by adding the Kansas City Royals and the Seattle Pilots, which later became the Milwaukee Brewers franchise. Meanwhile, the NL added the Montreal Expos, which became the Washington Nationals, and the San Diego Padres.

34. The Seattle Pilots moved to Milwaukee after just one season.

35. The four teams are the White Sox, Indians, Tigers, and Red Sox (although two of these teams, the Indians and the Red Sox, went through some nickname changes along the way).

36. The team we now know as the Reds were previously called the Cincinnati Red Stockings from 1882 through 1889. They also went by the Redlegs from 1954 through 1958. They've been the Reds in every other season they played. Incidentally, the nickname Reds began in 1890, but the change to Redlegs came about as a reaction to America's worries about the Red Scare. That is to say, the United States was deeply concerned about the influence of Communism in America and the fear of the Soviet Union's growing arsenal of nuclear weapons.

37. The two teams are the Braves franchise and the Athletics. The Braves began their existence in Boston (where they went by five different nicknames in the twentieth century), moved to Milwaukee in 1953, and found a home in Atlanta beginning in 1966. The franchise has, through 2020, won exactly three modern-era World Championships, one in each of their three cities. In most sources, the Braves are listed as the first major-league team ever to make a move from one city to another, seemingly ignoring the Orioles franchise. Meanwhile, the Athletics started off in Philadelphia in 1901, shifted to Kansas City from 1955 through 1967, then found a home in Oakland starting in 1968.

38. The Astros started off as the Houston Colt .45s. They kept that nickname from 1962 through 1964, when, what with the space race and the importance of that industry in Houston, they changed the name to Astros.

39. b. Atlanta, perhaps because some big-shot baseball executive flunked geography in grade school, was placed in the NL West in 1969. It wasn't until 1994, when baseball added a third division, that the Braves were put in the NL East. The answer to this question could not have possibly been "c," because that choice, the Central Division, as touched upon, didn't exist until '94.

40. In 1998, the Milwaukee Brewers were plucked from

the AL Central Division and moved to the NL Central. In 2013, the Astros went from its NL Central Division berth to the AL West.

41. The Reds hosted the first Opener each season for a baseball eternity. In 1939, the league officially gave permission to the Reds to start each year with the first home Opener beginning in 1940. One factor that altered that took place when baseball/television began scheduling some Openers on foreign soil, often a few days before other teams began play. The first time the Reds Opener was topped by a game played on foreign soil was in 2000 when the Chicago Cubs met the New York Mets in Tokyo, Japan, to start the major-league season.

One theory, disputed by some, has it that the Opening Day honor goes to Cincinnati because they were the first pro team, dating back to 1869. One constant has been the fact that since 1887 the Reds have begun every season at home, never on the road, with only five exceptions (such as delays in their first game due to rain).

One source states Cincinnati has been the host for "opening the Openers" from 1876 until the Opener in Japan in 1990. A different source has it that the only time that the Reds were actually scheduled to begin a season away from home was in 1888. That year they opened their schedule against the Kansas City Cowboys.

42. When Joe Musgrove threw his no-hitter vs. the Rangers on April 9, 2021, the San Diego Padres finally had one of their pitchers throw a no-no. It took them 8,206 regular-season contests to achieve this. Only one batter hit by a pitch prevented Musgrove, making only his second start as a Padre, from nailing down a perfect game. His gem was the first complete game of his 85 starts.

43. The catcher was Victor Caratini, which made him the first catcher in major-league history to work consecutive no-hitters for two different teams.

44. b. 1969. That year they won 100 games to top the Cubs by eight games to win the East Division. Then they swept the Braves in three games to win the pennant and went on to shock the Orioles in five to win it all. Tom Seaver and Company put away the O's of Frank and Brooks Robinson, Boog Powell, and 20-game-winners Mike Cuellar and Dave McNally (plus Jim Palmer) with relative ease, losing only the opener of the World Series.

45. 1970. Brooks Robinson took World Series MVP and not just for his glove work—he hit .429 with a couple of homers and six RBIs in five games.

46. c. 1934

47. The Los Angeles Dodgers. They defeated Don Drysdale twice and Sandy Koufax once, and remarkably held L.A. to just two runs, a new record, and 17 hits, meaning the Dodgers team batting average was a miserable .142! That measly batting average is the lowest ever by a team in World Series history. Baltimore needed just four pitchers, who combined for a stunning ERA of 0.50, to dispatch Los Angeles. It was just more evidence that pitching is what wins games. By the way, the total of 15 runs scored by both teams is the lowest ever in World Series competition. Final note—the Orioles scored more runs in one inning (of Game One) than Los Angeles scored for the entire Series.

48. The New York Giants of 1905

49. The Toronto Blue Jays. They were in their familiar home park, Rogers Centre in Toronto, to begin the 2019 season, but when COVID-19 hit, they were required to open the 2020 season using Sahlen Field in Buffalo for their home park. When 2021 rolled around, they played their Opener in TD Ballpark in Dunedin, Florida. The only other team to match this nomadic act was the Boston Braves from 1914 to 1916.

50. The Cleveland Indians. Despite their blazing streak and their 102 wins that season, Cleveland was upset in the ALDS by the Yankees. The Indians became a victim of a streak when New York bounced back from a two-games-to-none hole to win three in a row, finishing Cleveland off.

51. The New York Giants of 1916. They went from September 7 until the second game of a doubleheader on September 30 before losing a game. Their one tie was later replayed in its entirety even though it had reached the eighth inning before bad weather forced the contest to be called off.

The first win of their long run lifted their record to a mediocre 60–62, a remote 14 games out of first place.

Even though they won on September 7 to start their string of wins, the first-place Phillies swept a double-header that day so the Giants actually dropped 1/2 game in the standings. Plus they were a distant 11 games behind the third-place Boston Braves.

As impressive as their streak was, there were other elements of the skein that were also quite noteworthy. For example, despite winning 26 in a row, they failed to move up even one notch in the standings! Yes, the hot spell took them to 85–62, but the day the streak ended they were still in fourth place, five games out of first. They then finished the year seven games behind the pennant-winning Dodgers. The Giants had been planted in fourth place since July 27 and, though they neared a third-place berth, they never got there.

In fact, they not only finished the season in fourth place, they won only 86 games all year—and that's despite the fact that during the season they also rattled off a 17-game winning streak. Thus, 43 of their 86 total victories—exactly half—came from two spectacular winning streaks. Anyone learning these facts would have to surmise that this was a very good ball club, perhaps a pennant winner, certainly not a fourth-place team.

Want more? Their 17 wins in a row all came on the road. They won their first game of the road trip on May 9 and didn't lose until May 30. One last incredible fact is that their 26 in a row all came at home! Talk about a long home stand.

52. The Oakland A's

53. The Atlanta Braves. The team was on a 16-game

losing streak and Turner, it seems, planned on giving the squad's real manager, Dave Bristol, 10 days off so Turner could see up close what was going on with his team. His career managerial record was 0–1. Atlanta would win the next day, but regardless of who was managing, they were a very poor team, going 61–101 on the season. After losing his one game, Turner met with the media and made a point of showing them the check he had received that day for meal money.

54. Gene Autry. Although he didn't live long enough to see his team win the 2002 World Series, the team honored him as their 26th man by retiring that number. Autry owned the Angels from their inception through 1998.

55. The Yankees. The owner, of course, was George Steinbrenner. In a classic case of saying something which turned out to be far from true, in January of 1973, upon becoming the Yankees new owner, he uttered these words: "I won't be active in the day-to-day operations of the club at all."

56. The Houston Astros

57. The Yankees, to honor Lou Gehrig

58. Kapler was representing Ty Cobb, and in the days of Cobb, numbers weren't worn.

59. The Cleveland Indians. At first teams placed the numbers on jersey sleeves. A Hall of Fame website states that, finally, by the mid-1930s, all of the big-league teams outfitted their players with numbered uniforms. However, teams, wishing to sell scorecards to their home fans, often wore numbers only for away games. The 1937 Philadelphia Athletics were the first club to wear numbers at home and on the road.

60. The Dodgers

61. Los Angeles picked up Albert Pujols in May, adding him to their roster which included the 2018 AL MVP in Mookie Betts, the 2014 NL MVP, Clayton Kershaw, and the 2019 NL MVP, Cody Bellinger.

62. Ted Turner, who owned the Atlanta Braves

63. Baltimore fans shout the word "oh," doing so as a tribute to their O's, the Orioles.

64. Ebbets Field, home of the Brooklyn Dodgers

65. The Polo Grounds, home to the New York Giants

66. Wrigley Field in Chicago. Pitcher Dick Selma gets credit for stirring up the Bleacher Bums in '69 by waving a towel over his head one day, and the reputation of the Bums grew from then on.

67. The first version of Yankee Stadium was nicknamed The House That Ruth Built and it hosted its first game in 1923. A crowd of 74,000, then a big-league record, was on hand and they saw Babe Ruth fittingly christen the park with its first home run.

68. Atlanta's Fulton County Stadium, a hitter-friendly ballpark, was nicknamed the Launching Pad because homers seemingly flew out of there as if propelled by a howitzer.

69. The Orioles. They were just two losses shy of the all-time record for consecutive defeats set by the Phillies of 1961.

70. Casey Stengel. His team was so woeful at first that he was quoted as saying sarcastically, "Man will walk on the moon before the Mets ever win a World Series." Well, he was correct, but not really in the way he intended. Neil Armstrong made his moon walk a little less than three months before the Mets won the 1969 World Series.

71. Connie Mack. He led the Pirates from 1894 through 1986, then managed the Philadelphia Athletics from 1901 through 1950. He won 3,731 games and five World Championships over those years. He also lost 3,948 contests, but, as the outright or partial owner of the A's, he had great job security.

72. Tony La Russa, then with the White Sox. The victory that pushed him into second place still left him nearly 1,000 wins (967 exactly) behind Mack.

73. Chuck Tanner. He led the Bucs to a World Championship that season.

74. Sparky Anderson. A .218 hitter over the course of his one season of play, he won World Series in both leagues, five pennants, and nearly 2,200 games as a manager.

75. Cito Gaston

76. Bruce Bochy. When he retired after the 2019 season, his 2,003 wins ranked him no. 11 on the all-time managerial list. A small handful of big-leaguers were born in France, including Bochy, Steve Jeltz, and Charlie Lea.

77. Bochy, Connie Mack, Joe McCarthy, Casey Stengel, and Joe Torre

CHAPTER FOUR
MISCELLANEOUS ITEMS

1. Home Run: Who was the shortest man ever to appear in a big-league game?

2. Double: What two brothers combined for more lifetime home runs than any other brother act?

3. Home Run: What player, a four-time All-Star second baseman, was in the lineup for the Atlanta Braves the night Aaron broke the all-time home-run mark by launching homer no. 715, *and* two years later played in Japan during the game in which Sadaharu Oh also hit his 715th home run?

4. Single: In 2019, which power hitter set the new mark for the most homers hit by a rookie?

5. Single: For quite a few seasons, the Atlanta Braves had three future Hall of Fame pitchers in their starting rotation. Name them.

6. Double: For decades, the most sought after and expensive baseball card in existence was that of Honus Wagner. One of those rare 1909 cards went for $3.12 million in 2016. Then, in 2020, a Mike Trout–autographed rookie card, special but hardly an "antique" like Wagner's, sold for $3.93 million to shatter the Wagner record. Incredibly, less than one year later in early 2021, one baseball card went for an even higher price, an astronomical $5.2 million. Which player graced that card?

7. Triple: Which player chose to wear jersey no. 17 because that number, coupled with his last name, May, which also appeared on the back of his jersey, showed everyone his birthday? a. Carlos b. Lee c. Dave d. Rudy

8. Double: With which team did Sammy Sosa break into the majors? Stretch your double into a triple if you can name the future Hall of Famer he was traded for in 1989.

9. Double: If there was a record for the largest Afro by a big-leaguer, this man would claim that mark. Clue: his last name, as a verb, is a baseball taboo.

10. Single: Which lefty spent more years with Houston than the other clubs that he was with (such as the Mets)? Despite a small frame, 5'10", he could top the 100 mph mark. He wound up with more than 400 saves, still in the top 10 all-time (no. 6 through 2021).

11. Double: Now, *this* relief ace went just 5'8" but set a record in 1959 for the highest single-season winning percentage ever (18–1, .947 WL%).

12. Single: This BYU athlete played in the majors for Toronto, and in the NBA mainly for the Boston Celtics.

As a big-leaguer he hit just .220 and had a negative lifetime WAR (-2.0), but he was an NBA All-Star who averaged 11.5 points per game for 14 seasons.

13. Home Run: What was the last team Mike Piazza played for, serving as a designated hitter there?

14. Single: In 2019, Toronto had three rookies whose fathers played in the majors. Name the Blue Jay whose father, a Hall of Famer, collected 3,000 hits, all with Houston.

15. Single: The father, also a Hall of Famer, of the next Toronto rookie from 2019 starred with the Expos and Angels and was known for being able to hit pitches crisply, even those way outside the strike zone. Name the Blue Jay in question.

16. Double: The third father, part of the Blake Street Bombers, starred mainly with Colorado where he led the league in hits, homers (40), and RBIs (128) in 1995. Identify his son.

17. Double: The next several questions concern which team the listed players were with when they collected their 3,000th hit. Start with this: name the club *either* Eddie Murray or Ichiro Suzuki was with for their milestone hit.

18. Triple: Rickey Henderson—this one's tough because he suited up for nine major-league clubs.

19. Double: Wade Boggs

20. Single: Adrian Beltre

21. Single: Paul Molitor

22. Home Run: Which pitcher served up Tris Speaker's 3,000th hit and a record-setting homer in 1927 (mentioned in Chapter Two)?

23. Home Run: Which pitcher, famous for his eephus pitch, gave up Paul Waner's 3,000th hit and a memorable All-Star Game homer off his blooper pitch to Ted Williams—the only home run ever off that high arcing, odd offering?

24. Home Run: There have been other pitchers who gained some fame throwing a high arcing pitch. Clue: two of these men had special names given to their odd pitches, the folly floater and the LaLob. Your job is to name one of the two players referred to here.

25. Home Run: Who was the first player to take home the All-Star Game MVP trophy for a game played in his home park (in 1997)?

26. Single: In 1994, the Indians lineup was so explosive these two (young at the time) power hitters batted in the eighth and/or ninth slot in the lineup a combined 58 times. Plus, the next year one of them hit either sixth, seventh, or eighth 104 times while the other was in the no. six or no. seven hole 118 times. Name either man.

27. Double: The Blake Street Bombers were mentioned in question 16. Name two to earn a double. Take credit for a homer if you can name all five of the Rockies who are considered to be the original Blake Street Bombers.

28. Double: What Braves first baseman set a since-broken record in 1954 when he annihilated four pitches for homers and added a double for 18 total bases in one game? He also came up with the only hit, the game winner, during the 1959 contest in which Harvey Haddix threw 12 perfect innings.

The answers to the next seven questions will have something to do with a color.

29. For a Double: Who broke the 18 total bases record by drilling four homers, a double, plus a single in a 2002 outburst?

30. Single: Name the former pitcher who managed the Padres from 2007 through part of 2015 then was hired by the Rockies in 2017. He was the Angels pitching coach when they won it all in 2002.

31. Double: This outfielder was one of a handful of bright spots during some of the lean Yankee years from the latter part of the 1960s and into the 1970s. Several times he led the team in WAR.

32. Single: He was a southpaw pitcher who burst onto the scene with Oakland in 1971, leading the league with a microscopic ERA of 1.82 and a towering total of 301 strikeouts.

33. Single: Name the man whose real first name is Daniel, but who was mainly known by a nickname that relates to an orangish-red color (the color of his hair). When he played in Montreal, he gained a nickname that tied in with a color and with the French language—Le Grand Orange.

34. Double: Most associated with the Cardinals as a second baseman and a successful coach and manager who won the 1967 World Series, the first name this man went by was a primary color.

35. Double: Name the pitcher who spent most of his 19 seasons with Texas and the Dodgers, and who earned a World Series ring with the '97 Marlins. He led his league in ERA twice.

36. Double: The youngest player to reach 300 homers was Mel Ott in 1931 at the age of 22 years and 132 days. Two other men hit their 300th home run before the age of 23—name the one who, like Ott, went on to hit 500+ HRs.

37. Double: Name the other man who matched Ott. Clue: he was mainly a Boston outfielder, and his career was cut short when he was beaned, leading to a severe eye injury.

38. Single: The 2020 season was a short one, so there

were even fewer nine-inning complete-game shutouts than usual of late. How many were there? a. 2 b. 5 c. 11

39. Single: When Pete Rose retired who, in 1987, became the active major-league leader for lifetime hits? Clue: this Dodgers first baseman had 1,657 fewer hits than Rose, but he was, nevertheless, the active leader at that point.

40. Single: Despite allegations of PED use, this man took a job with Fox to provide baseball analysis. Clue: he is a three-time MVP winner who primarily spent his career playing on the left side of the diamond. Trivia note: he did some DH'ing and actually started one game at first base.

41. Single: Several clubs also hired people despite their having been associated with PEDs, thus tainting some memorable feats by stars of the past and the very game of baseball itself. One such player, a record-setting slugger, was first hired by the Cardinals as a coach. Another was also a longball hitter, a man who was infamous for his unpredictable ways. He became a player-coach in the Cubs minor-league system. Name either man.

42. Home Run: Warning—this question is almost unfair, so you should either think way, *way* outside the box, or give up, look at the answer, then either grumble or groan in disgust. Through 2020, who was the last switch-hitting AL player to win the MVP Award?

43. Double: Tough question, but if you've read enough

about baseball history, you had to have come across this tragic event. Who is the only big-league player ever to die as a result of an on-the-field incident? The player, on the 1920 Cleveland Indians, died the day after being hit in the head by a pitch. Who is this man?

44. Triple: What submarine pitcher threw the pitch that killed the player in the previous question?

45. Home Run: In 2006, a Yankees pitcher and his certified flight instructor were killed when his small airplane crashed into the side of a building in New York City.

46. Home Run: The NL 1962 Rookie of the Year, who also won a Gold Glove for his play at second base for the Cubs, also died as a result of a plane crash. The 1963 season was one that fit in the sophomore jinx department for him as he slumped to a .235 batting average. It would be his final season because his fatal crash took place during the offseason. Who is this player?

47. Double: More tragedy. This one ended in murder. The player in question had a four-season career in the majors spent with the Twins and, in his last year, 1978, with the Angels. He owned a lifetime batting average of .311 and once hit as high as .336—that was the year he came in second for the batting crown, trailing only teammate Rod Carew, who sizzled with a .388 batting average. The future looked glowing for the player being discussed here until a shotgun blast ended his life. Name this man.

48. Single: Which ballpark named one of its streets Vin Scully Avenue, giving Scully the honor in 2016, his final season as the team's longtime broadcaster?

49. Single: Which park once had the address of 4 Yawkey Way, but that address is now Jersey Street?

50. Single: Which classic, old ballpark sits between these streets: Addison, Clark, Waveland, and Sheffield?

51. Double: Which long-gone ballpark sat next to Bedford Avenue, Sullivan Place, McKeever Place, and Montgomery Street? Slight clue: the last game played there took place in 1957.

52. Single: Which big-league venue is the oldest one still in use in the majors, as of 2021?

53. Single: What is the second oldest park in the NL, as of 2021?

54. Triple: On June 2, 2010, a Detroit Tigers pitcher threw a perfect game—only it wasn't a perfect game. Explanation: What should have been the 27th consecutive out came when Cleveland's Jason Donald hit a grounder to first. The pitcher covered the bag and, as replays *clearly* showed, took the throw to conclude his gem. However, the first-base ump absolutely blew the call and the perfecto vanished like a puff of smoke. With no replay rule in place to challenge the call back then, the call stood. Surprisingly, almost shocking, the pitcher then simply smiled and went back to work, retiring the next batter. Name the pitcher involved.

55. Home Run: Now you must identify the first-base umpire.

56. Single: True or false—the 2000 World Series was played entirely in just one city.

57. Single: True or false—the 1944 World Series was played in just one city, *and* in just one ballpark.

58. Triple: Several men have strung together torrid streaks in which they hit a home run in eight consecutive games, good for an all-time record. Who was the first player to do this? Clue: he did this with the Pirates in 1956.

59. Single: Who was the next man to accomplish this home-run splurge? Like the man from the previous question, this player was mainly a first baseman.

60. Single: To wrap up this frequently mentioned record, what outfielder became the third man to put together such a home-run spree?

61. Home Run: This is a tough one. A six-year veteran of the majors, this lifetime .212 hitter moved on to play pro ball in Japan where he became one of their greats. He was, in fact, that league's highest paid player, earning more than $1 million at one point. Clues: he was a first baseman who spent the bulk of his big-league days with the Padres. His last name is the same as a type of fish.

62. Double: The second player to earn $1 million or more in Japan was another American, a .281 hitter who spent all but one of his 10 seasons with the Montreal Expos. There he was at times joined in the outfield by stars such as Ellis Valentine, Andre Dawson, and Tim Raines. Name this player.

63. Single: Which former President of the United States played in the first two College World Series in 1947 and 1948, acting as the captain of his Yale squad?

64. Home Run: The next nine questions contain this common thread—the first nine times players won back-to-back MVP Awards, those nine men each played a different position. In other words, you could construct a team based on the first group of players to win consecutive MVPs, an incredible coincidence. Begin with the pitcher. He accomplished this as a member of the Tigers in 1944 and 1945.

65. Single: Next comes the catcher who did this in 1954 and 1955.

66. Double: The first baseman was a true slugger who won his successive MVPs in 1932 and 1933.

67. Single: A key member of the Big Red Machine was sensational at second base as he copped back-to-back MVP trophies in 1975 and 1976.

68. Double: The shortstop was a member of the Chicago Cubs when he managed the feat in 1958 and 1959.

69. Single: At third base was the man who may well be the greatest third sacker of all time. The powerful Philadelphia Phillie won the MVP in 1980 and 1981 (and another one in 1986).

70. Single: One of the outfielders played for the Braves at the height of their WTBS-TV coverage as America's Team. His twin MVPs came in 1982 and 1983.

71. Single: This man is the second of three Yankees on our list. He won MVP Awards in 1956, 1957, and threw in another for good measure in 1962. Name this center fielder.

72. Single: Speaking of 1962, this right fielder won his consecutive MVPs in the two years prior to '62, doing so as a Yankees teammate to the man from the previous question.

73. Single: After the nine men discussed above, four other players have won back-to-back MVP trophies. Name one of them. Clue: some of these men are mentioned elsewhere in this book.

74. Single: On April 15, baseball celebrates Jackie Robinson Day each year to commemorate the anniversary of the day he broke into the big leagues. Every major leaguer wears his number, 42, to honor the man who broke baseball's color barrier. When baseball decided to do this, they decreed that no player could ever again wear number 42 in the majors—it was to be permanently retired by all big-league clubs. However, a ruling stated that if a player was wearing no. 42 at the time the decision was made to honor Robinson, those men could continue to wear that jersey number until, of course, they retired. Who was the last big-leaguer, a future Hall of Fame pitcher, to wear 42?

75. Double: Which venerable ballpark features a foul pole with its own name, Pesky's Pole?

76. Single: Which other venerable park, this one in the NL, has the words, "Hey, Hey," marked on its foul poles?

77. Single: When the Globe Theatre in London was the site for many of William Shakespeare's plays, an eon before people were notified of entertainment news via radio, television, and the internet, potential theater-go-ers would learn that a play was to be performed on given days by the flying of a flag over the Globe. A white flag was used to indicate a comedy was being put on, a black flag was used for a tragedy, and a red flag flying meant the day's play was a history play.

Today fans can use a similar means of communication if they travel near a certain ballpark to learn if the home team had won or lost a game. A victory is indicated by the flying of a white flag adorned by a blue "W" rippling over the park. A white "L" on a blue flag, of course, reveals the bad news to, say, commuters traveling home on the nearby elevated train track. Which ballpark has done this for years?

78. Single: Which NL team has a giant replica of the glove worn by their most famous player, a man who could slug the ball as well as he could run them down?

79. Double: What legendary college program, which began under Bobby Winkles in 1959, produced such big-leaguers as Reggie Jackson, Sal Bando, Larry Gura, Gary Gentry, Lenny Randle, Craig Swan, and Lerrin LaGrow?

80. Home Run: What other player from Winkles's program not only went on to become a big-league All-Star who made trivia fame as the first overall pick in baseball's first Free Agent Amateur Draft in 1965 when the Kansas City Athletics chose him?

81. Single: What other college became known as a baseball factory under their legendary coach Rod Dedeaux? His West Coast teams churned out stars by the dozens.

82. Single: On April 26, 2021, an AL player did something nobody had done in almost exactly 100 years. The man in question matched a feat Babe Ruth did on June 13, 1921, when he made a start as a pitcher while also perching atop the majors in home runs. Name this versatile player.

83. Single: The man who is the answer to the previous

question went 4–2 over 51 2/3 innings pitches and tossed in 22 homers in his rookie season. Who was the last player before him to work 50+ innings while also compiling 20 or more home runs in the same season?

84. Double: Dwight Gooden, the winner of 194 games and a man who won a Cy Young Award in his second season after taking the 1984 Rookie of the Year Award, was the uncle of a famous slugger. Clue: his nephew owns 509 lifetime home runs, and both of them attended Hillsborough High School in Tampa, Florida.

85. Triple: Roy Smalley was with the Minnesota Twins for most of the 1976 season through early 1982. From 1976 through 1980, his manager for all but 36 games was his uncle. Name the uncle who also managed the Phillies, Expos, and finished his managerial days with the Angels.

86. Home Run: A shortstop joined the Washington Senators in 1928 after he had spent some time with the Pittsburgh Pirates. In Washington, he met the niece of team owner Clark Griffith. After the 1934 season ended, he married the girl, Mildred Robertson. Name her husband, the young future Hall of Famer.

87. Single: Through 2021, the Colorado Rockies had retired the jersey number of just two players. One was a powerful outfielder while the other man was a good stick/good glove infielder. Name either player.

88. Single: Through 2020, the Arizona D-backs have

also been judicious about retiring their players' numbers. They have honored just two men—name either for a single, or stretch it to two bases if you can identify both players.

89. Single: Same question, but this time for the Seattle Mariners—name one of two men honored by the M's to earn a single, or both for a two-base hit.

90. Double: Through 2020, only one team has yet to retire the jersey of any of its players, although one man who passed away while still an active player (in 2016) was given consideration for this honor.

91. Double: What All-Star and Gold Glove–winning catcher wore the unusual number "09" on his back for several years with the Padres and Marlins? Clue: he was the NL Rookie of the Year in 1987.

92. Home Run: If you get this one, you're good! If you miss it, add it to your knowledge of trivia from here on. Which pitcher who mainly played for the New York Giants in the 1940s wore uniform no. 96 because that was the actual name of the town where he was raised, Ninety Six, South Carolina?

93. Single: There once was a minor-league player who intentionally had the numeral sewn on his jersey *flipped over*. That is to say, the numeral was turned 180 degrees from the normal position. He did that because his last name, when read backwards, was a one-digit number. That might not have looked so odd if he had worn no.

1, and no. 8 would look fine regardless. At any rate, what was this man's last name? a. Owt b. Rouf c. Neves d. Enin

94. Double: Sean Kazmar Jr. went 12 years and 206 days between big-league appearances, from what had been his last game in 2008 to a pinch-hitting appearance in 2021. Name either of the two men who, from 1950 on, had gone the longest period of time without playing in a major-league game. Clues: one was an ageless pitcher, the other one played in five different decades.

95. Single: True or false—at one point long ago, a runner was given credit for a stolen base if he advanced more than one base on a hit, or if he moved up a base on a caught fly ball.

96. Single: True or false—at one time, essentially what we now know as a ground rule double on any fair ball that bounces over the fence was ruled a home run.

97. Single: True or false—long ago, there was a rule that stated that a batter could indicate to the pitcher whether he wanted the ball to be thrown to him high or low (not inside or outside, though).

98. Triple: Who was the first man (and, through 2021, the only one) to put up a season with 50 or more doubles and homers? a. Ted Williams b. Babe Ruth c. Albert Belle d. Mo Vaughn

99. Home Run: Mel Ott has just six letters in the full

name he went by, but a catcher who spent 1974 through 1981 in the majors went by a name that contained just five letters. Name him.

100. Home Run: Prior to 1900, it wasn't extremely rare to see a left-handed throwing catcher in a big-league game. In the modern era, though, one source states that there have only been a handful of such men, *and* only three of them have caught since 1958. Name any one of those left-handed throwing catchers.

101. Double: On May 4, 1975, a first baseman for the Houston Astros scored the 1,000,000th run in big-league history. Clue: he is a member of the Astros Hall of Fame. Name him.

102. Double: Who scored major-league baseball's 2,000,000th run on May 29, 2021? Clues: he did this with the Twins, but his greatest claim to fame was winning the 2015 AL MVP with Toronto.

103. Single: True or false—when Albert Pujols won the 2001 Rookie of the Year Award, he started 30+ games at first base, third base, left field, and right field.

104. Single: As mentioned in Chapter Three, Davey Johnson once hit 43 HRs in a season. What was his next highest total? a. 10 b. 18 c. 41

105. Single: Similar question. Brady Anderson broke into the majors in 1988. His highest season home-run

total through 1995 was 21. How many did he hit in '96?
a. 50 b. 21 c. 13

106. Double: Six rookies have led their league in home runs. Two are obscure players from baseball's spider-webbed distant past, men who led with just nine and 12 homers, but the other four are big-name players. Name any two of these men.

107. Home Run: This slugger played for four teams from all four of the then-existing four divisions in 1977, a first. Name him.

108. Home Run: Here's a question that was once a popular trivia challenge—who is the only man to pinch-hit for Ted Williams?

109. Home Run: Only six men ever pinch-hit for Hank Aaron. Name the one who did this the most often when he was with Aaron in Atlanta.

110. Home Run: These are tough questions (this one should be worth an automatic grand slam), but great trivia items to add to your knowledge of baseball lore. Who acquired the nickname "Babe Ruth's Legs" because when Ruth was in his last several seasons, the man in question often pinch-ran and/or replaced Ruth in the field?

CHAPTER FOUR ANSWERS: MISCELLANEOUS ITEMS

1. Eddie Gaedel, who stood 3'7" and who wore jersey number "1/8" when he went to the plate in what may be baseball's most famous publicity stunt, one engineered by team owner Bill Veeck, a true baseball maverick. Gaedel drew a walk on four pitches and was pulled from the game for a pinch-runner, never again to appear in the batter's box, banned by a hastily drawn-up baseball rule.

2. The Aarons. Hank belted 755 homers and his brother Tommie added 13, giving them a seemingly insurmountable total of 768 career home runs.

3. Davey Johnson. In Aaron's record-breaking contest, Johnson was two slots behind Aaron in the lineup, and he was the on-deck hitter in Oh's historic game. For the record, Oh is credited with having hit more professional homers lifetime, 868, than any other pro player.

4. Pete Alonso with 53, which led the majors that year.

5. Greg Maddux, John Smoltz, and Tom Glavine. They were with the Braves as a trio from 1993 through 2002.

6. Mickey Mantle. The card, called the Holy Grail of the trading industry, was his 1952 Topps card. That record has since been surpassed. For example, a Babe Ruth card, valued at more than $6 million, sold for a reported new undisclosed record later in 2021. In fact, by mid-August of 2021, the Wagner card was again back on top after it sold for $6,606,000. When the spiral ends is anyone's guess.

7. a. Carlos May

8. Sosa was a rookie with Texas. He was traded for Harold Baines.

9. Oscar Gamble

10. Billy Wagner

11. Roy Face. All of his 18 wins in 1959 came out of the bullpen. It's almost unbelievable, but he finished several seasons weighing just 146 pounds. Over a stretch from late in 1958 through his first 17 wins in 1959, Face won 22 games in a row, 10 in extra innings. He went 97 straight games without a loss. In a 2019 interview, Face stated matter of factly, "I don't think anybody's going to be 18–1 again."

12. Danny Ainge. With Toronto, he finished in last place in each of his three big-league seasons. With the Celtics, he was an NBA champ twice.

13. Oakland A's

14. Cavan Biggio, son of Craig

15. Vladimir Guerrero Jr.

16. Bo Bichette, son of Dante

17. Murray was with Cleveland; Ichiro was a Marlin

18. The Padres—did you remember he even played briefly for teams such as the Dodgers, Angels, Red Sox, M's, and Blue Jays?

19. The Rays

20. The Rangers

21. The Twins

22. Tom Zachary, the man who gave up Ruth's 60th homer in '27

23. Rip Sewell, the cousin of Hall of Famer Joe Sewell, mentioned elsewhere in this book

24. Steve Hamilton and Dave LaRoche. One source also lists other men to throw an eephus pitch, including Bill Lee, who was tagged for a Tony Perez homer off that pitch in the 1975 World Series, Luis Tiant, Pascual Perez, Zack Greinke, Clayton Kershaw, Livan Hernandez, and Pedro Borbon.

25. Sandy Alomar in Cleveland

26. Jim Thome and Manny Ramirez

27. Dante Bichette, Ellis Burks, Vinny Castilla, Larry Walker, and Andres Galarraga

28. Joe Adcock

29. Shawn Green

30. Bud Black

31. Roy White

32. Vida Blue. Trivia sidenote: The owner of Blue's first team, the Oakland Athletics, was Charley Finley, an over-the-top, colorful promoter. In 1971, Finley actually offered Blue a bonus if he'd change his first name to "True." Wanting no part of a True Blue moniker, the pitcher refused.

33. Rusty Staub, one of the most popular Expos ever. He also happened to be a gourmet chef and wine expert.

34. Hall of Famer Red Schoendienst

35. Kevin Brown

36. Eddie Mathews, who wound up with one career homer more than Ott, who hit 511.

37. Tony Conigliaro

38. b. 5

39. Steve Garvey

40. Alex Rodriguez, who also was hired by ESPN. Fox also hired the suspended-for-life (for gambling on baseball) Pete Rose to work in their studios.

For that matter, Miami blundered by hiring Barry Bonds as their hitting coach for the 2016 season. The team president at the time, David Samson, was quoted in a *Sports Illustrated* article as calling the hiring of Bonds a "complete disaster." He called Bonds "combative" and revealed that Bonds demanded a salary of $1.5 million, much higher than the pay other big-league hitting coaches got. "It was all about Barry," Samson added. "We had to do so many special things for him in terms of how we traveled, the hotel and the suite and the food, the money. It was an absolute nightmare." Furthermore, Samson said that no player improved because of Bonds. The Marlins finished the season 13th out of 15 teams for runs scored and next to last for homers.

41. Mark McGwire (who also coached for the Dodgers and Padres) and Manny Ramirez

42. Vida Blue was a switch-hitter and he earned his MVP trophy, albeit for his pitching prowess, in 1971. That season, his first full year in the majors, he turned the baseball world agog, becoming one of the rare pitchers to win the MVP and the Cy Young Award in the same season. He went 24–8 on the year. As for his hitting ability, in 1971 he went 12-for-102, and lifetime he hit .104.

43. Ray Chapman

44. Carl Mays of the Yankees

45. Cory Lidle. The 34-year-old Lidle was the third flying-related fatality in Yankees history, following Thurman Munson and Jim Hardin, who spent 12 games as a Yankee and passed away 19 years after he retired from the Braves. Lidle was coming off his one season as a Yankee, dying four days after the 2006 season ended when the Tigers eliminated New York from postseason play.

46. Ken Hubbs, who was only 22 years old at the time of his accident. He broke into the majors briefly at the age of just 19. Hubbs was the first rookie ever to win a Gold Glove. He even set records by playing in the most straight errorless games, 78, and handling the most successive chances without a mishap ever by a second baseman. Hubbs was at the stick of his new Cessna 172 when the accident occurred.

More recently (in 2017), Hall of Famer Roy Halladay died after losing control of his plane while performing what was called extreme acrobatics as he flew his small propeller plane, crashing into the Gulf of Mexico.

47. Lyman Bostock. He was shot by a jealous husband who mistakenly thought Bostock was involved with his wife. In fact, the wife was the target of the husband's shot. One report said Bostock had just met the woman on the day he was killed, and knew her for just twenty minutes. Incidentally, Bostock's father, Lyman Sr., was a batting champ once in the Negro Leagues.

48. This one was probably too easy—the answer is Dodger Stadium, and Scully, of course, was their superlative, legendary announcer. The official address for the park is now 1000 Vin Scully Avenue.

49. Boston's Fenway Park. The Yawkey Way name was dropped because it was named after longtime Red Sox owner Tom Yawkey, a man who was alleged to be a racist. For example, critics pointed out, among other things, the fact that Yawkey did not integrate the Red Sox with a Black player until Pumpsie Green joined the team in late July of 1959, more than 12 years after Jackie Robinson broke baseball's color barrier. The Red Sox were, in fact, the last major-league club to have a Black player on its squad.

Trivia sidenote—Pumpsie Green is the brother of Dallas Cowboys star defensive back Cornell Green, a man who was voted to five Pro Bowls.

50. Wrigley Field, home field of the Chicago Cubs since 1916

51. Ebbets Field, home of the Brooklyn Dodgers

52. Fenway Park. It is four years older than Wrigley Field. Fenway opened on April 20, 1912. The big news about the new facility was overshadowed by the continuing fascination and newspaper coverage of the sinking of the Titanic, which took place five days earlier.

53. Dodger Stadium. A mere toddler compared to Fenway and Wrigley, Dodger Stadium is nevertheless old by NL standards, having made its debut in 1962.

54. The forgiving, understanding pitcher was Armando Galarraga. Some writers dubbed his gem as a 28-out perfect game. People have speculated that Galarraga's *not* getting his perfect game in such a sad and dramatic way makes him more memorable than if he had gotten the call at first base. Whether you got this question right or not, addresses that theory. Another thing, if he had earned the perfect game, it would have been the second in the majors in less than a week because Roy Halladay had thrown one just four days earlier.

Galarraga's record after his flirtation with perfection was 2–1, but he went 2–8 over the rest of the 2010 season. His big-league days ended in 2012 with a career mark of 26–34, with one of those wins being historic.

55. The contrite umpire, Jim Joyce, knew he had muffed the call. He apologized profusely to Galarraga and then later wrote a book with Galarraga entitled *Nobody's Perfect*.

56. True. This took place when the Mets and Yankees met in the World Series in New York City. This occurrence was known as the Subway Series. When the New York Giants and the Brooklyn Dodgers were still playing in the City, and the Yankees often won pennants, a Subway Series was hardly rare. There were 13 World Series involving two of those teams with each game, of course, being held in New York. Going way back, the

1906 World Series was also played in one city, Chicago. On that occasion most of the media called the matchup the Crosstown Series.

57. True. Both the St. Louis Cardinals and the Browns used Sportsman's Park as their home base, so when those two teams won pennants in 1944, each of the games in the World Series took place there.

In 1921 and 1922, the New York Giants and Yankees met in the Series with all of the games being held at the Polo Grounds. Some writers, especially from a long ago era, referred to any World Series held in the same city as a Trolley Series. That was the case, for example, with the 1944 Series, although some labeled that event as the Streetcar Series.

Due to the COVID-19 pandemic, the entire World Series contest of 2020 was played at Globe Life Field in Arlington, Texas, the usual home of the Rangers.

58. Dale Long

59. In 1987, Yankees star Don Mattingly tied Long's record.

60. It's hard to believe that three men could get so hot as to hit homers in eight straight games, but in 1993, Ken Griffey Jr. joined this exclusive club.

61. Randy Bass. In Japan he won back-to-back Triple Crowns in 1985 and 1986 when his combined home-run total was 101. In 1986, he hit a personal high of

.389, and his career batting average overseas was .337, or 125 points higher than what he hit in the States.

Bass experienced some anti-American sentiment in Japan. When Bass played in the season finale of 1985, he was one home run shy of Sadaharu Oh's single-season record. Bass's opponent that day was the Tokyo Giants managed by Oh. Bass was issued four intentional walks to thwart his bid for the home-run record. The only time he put his bat on the ball came after he had been intentionally walked twice. In desperation, knowing he would get nothing good to hit all day long, he reached way across the plate just to make contact with the ball, but all he could muster was a single.

62. Warren Cromartie

63. George H. W. Bush. His lifetime batting average in collegiate play was .224.

64. This one is probably the toughest one of the nine men. It was Hal Newhouser.

65. Yogi Berra

66. Jimmie Foxx when he was with the Philadelphia Athletics

67. Joe Morgan

68. Ernie Banks. Many fans remember him as a first baseman, but he did play shortstop early in his career, and that's where he was when he won his MVP Awards.

69. Mike Schmidt

70. Dale Murphy. He can be placed in left field (where he spent 101 games in all) if the goal is to represent all nine positions rather than simply have three outfielders count as one general position. In all honesty, though, he mainly was stationed in center field and he did play right field quite a bit.

71. Mickey Mantle

72. Roger Maris

73. Barry Bonds (1992 and 1993; also in 2001 through 2004), Frank Thomas (1993 and 1994), Albert Pujols (2008 and 2009), and Miguel Cabrera (2012 and 2013)

74. Reliever Mariano Rivera, who was grandfathered into wearing no. 42 until he left the game in 2013

75. Boston's Fenway Park. One source says Red Sox star shortstop Johnny Pesky didn't have much power, but he did hit some of his six Fenway homers (and just 17 total lifetime homers) near, and even curving *around* the park's right-field foul pole.

76. Chicago's Wrigley Field. The words on the poles are in reference to a catch phrase used by longtime Cubs play-by-play announcer Jack Brickhouse. The words were added to the foul poles in 1999, the year after Brickhouse's passing.

77. Wrigley Field. The white flag flies from the left-field side of the scoreboard, the "L" signal on the right-field side. If Chicago split a doubleheader, both flags are on display. There is also a blue light that shines for a win and a white light which is lit to indicate a Cubs loss.

78. The San Francisco Giants. The glove is modeled after the one worn by Willie Mays, a defender so good writers came up with many gems to describe him. One wit said Mays's glove is where triples go to die. After one of his deep blasts, a writer came up with the line, "The only man who could have caught that ball just hit it."

79. Arizona State University. Under Winkles, who also managed the California Angels and the Oakland Athletics, the Sun Devils won national titles in 1965, 1967, and 1969. The college also produced Bob Horner, Floyd Bannister, Ken Landreaux, Hubie Brooks, Mike Devereaux, Barry Bonds, and Oddibe McDowell. In fact, the final three men from above made up the out-field for the 1984 ASU team, with Bonds and McDowell making the All-Tournament team for that year's College World Series.

80. Rick Monday

81. The University of Southern California. Some of the big-name players USC sent to the majors include Ron Fairly, Don Buford, Tom Seaver, Randy Johnson, Mark McGwire, Dave Kingman, Barry Zito, Steve Kemp, Bill Lee, Fred Lynn, and Bret and Aaron Boone. In fact, Dedeaux coached more than 50 players who went on to the majors. He retired in 1986 at the age of 72 after coaching for 45 seasons. He left the game as the winningest coach in college baseball history with a record of 1,332–571 and a fantastic 11 College World Series titles to his credit.

82. Shohei Ohtani. The 2018 AL Rookie of the Year was tied with seven other players for the home-run lead early in the year (7 HRs) when he made his start vs. the Rangers. He struck out nine in his five-inning start, gave up four earned runs, and earned his first victory of 2021. At the plate, he went 2-for-3 with two runs driven in and three runs scored. The games' box score took on a peculiar appearance with the pitcher hitting in the number two slot in the order.

Ohtani, despite an unimpressive 3–1 record in early July of 2021, was named to the All-Star squad as a pitcher. He was also named to the team as an outfielder, and he was on board for the Home Run Derby as well.

By 1921, when Ruth achieved this feat, his pitching days were nearly over. He was on the mound only twice that year, and he would not pitch again, in one game, until 1930. He then made one final start in 1933 as a sort of gate attraction in a meaningless game on the last day of the Yankees season. So, at the age of 38, Ruth shook off any mound rustiness he had and went the distance against his former team, the Red Sox. He did give up 12 hits and five earned runs, but went the route and got the win, taking his lifetime record to 94–46, which translates to a marvelous winning percentage of .671.

83. Babe Ruth. In 1919, he threw 133 1/3 innings and registered a record of 9–5 to go with his 29 home runs.

84. Gary Sheffield, who is only four years and two days younger than his uncle

85. Gene Mauch

86. Joe Cronin. By the way, his "marriage" to the Senators ended around the time his wedding took place—no preferential treatment from his wife's uncle. Griffith traded Cronin in late October of 1934 to the Red Sox for a shortstop named Lyn Lary, who lasted just 39 games with the Senators. However, Washington also received a fortune for Cronin, a then eye-popping amount of $225,000, a record at the time. It's odd, but with Cronin as their player/manager, the team won the AL pennant in 1933; then, without him, they would not win another flag until 1965 after the team had moved to Minnesota.

87. Larry Walker and Todd Helton

88. Luis Gonzalez and Randy Johnson

89. Edgar Martinez and Ken Griffey Jr.

90. The Florida/Miami Marlins. They have honored Jose Fernandez, who died in a boating accident in 2016, but not by officially retiring his no. 16 (even though no Marlin has worn that number since Fernandez's death). Trivia note: the year he died, he had already made 29

starts and sported a 16–8 record. He earned 18 vote points (one second, one third, one fourth, and nine fifth-place votes) in the Cy Young Award balloting. Only he and Lyman Bostock (for MVP consideration) ever received votes for a significant award posthumously.

91. Benito Santiago. He said that if he just wore no. 9, when he squatted behind the plate the numeral would be obscured by the strap on the back of his chest protector which ran down the middle of his shirt—and through his no. 9—on his uniform. Adding the "0" solved that problem.

92. Bill Voiselle

93. Johnny Neves wore a backwards "7" on his jersey in his only season, 1951, while playing for the Fargo-Moorhead Twins in the Northern League. So the answer is c. Look this up to see how peculiar this looks.

94. The pitcher is Satchel Paige. The five-decade player is Minnie Minoso, who played in the 1940s, 1950s, 1960s, and, as a promotion, in three games in 1976 (he went 1-for-8) and two contests in 1980 at the age of 54.

95. True. These stolen-base rules date back to the pre-1900 era, and they didn't last very long.

96. True. The ground rule double rule came along in 1929 in the AL and 1931 in the NL. Prior to that, balls that bounced into the stands were declared home runs.

97. True. That rule was put into effect in 1867 and, of course, didn't stay on the books for more than two decades.

98. c. Belle. He hit 50 HRs and 52 doubles and did so in just 143 games during a strike-shortened 1995 season.

99. Ed Ott, who was not related to Mel. Trivia note: Mel Ott is the only modern-era Hall of Famer whose last initial is "O."

100. Dale Long did this for two games in 1958. Mike Squires did it twice in 1980 (and he retired the final batter his team faced as a pitcher in 1984). The last left-handed throwing catcher in the majors was in 1989 when Benny Distefano appeared in three games behind the plate.

101. Bob Watson. Trivia note: Watson appeared in the movie *The Bad News Bears in Breaking Training* and had one speaking line.

102. Josh Donaldson

103. True. In fact, he started games in the outfield more times, 71, than at first base (31) or third base (52).

104. b. 18

105. a. 50

106. Pete Alonso (who was mentioned earlier in this

chapter), Aaron Judge, Mark McGwire, Ralph Kiner, Tim Jordan (12 HRs in 1906), and Harry Lumley (nine homers in 1904).

107. Dave Kingman. He began 1977 with the Mets before moving on to play with the Padres, Angels, and Yankees.

108. Carroll Hardy. In a 1960 contest, Williams fouled a ball off his foot and had to be replaced by Hardy, who hit into a double play. Just eight days later, after Williams homered in his final at bat, and after Williams trotted out to take his position in left field where he basked in the cheers and adulation of the Boston fans, the Red Sox manager sent Hardy out to play the field for the ninth inning, to replace Williams for the last time.

One source states Hardy is also the only man to pinch-hit for Carl Yastrzemski; and he hit his first big-league homer while pinch-hitting for Roger Maris.

109. Mike Lum. The Hawaiian-born outfielder was the first American with a Japanese ancestry to make it to the majors. The first man to pinch-hit for Aaron was Lee Maye, a man who also carved out a successful career as a doo-wop/R & B singer (not to be confused with slugger Lee May). After Maye came Johnny Blanchard, Lum, John Briggs, Marty Perez, and Mike Hegan.

110. Sammy Byrd. He is the only man ever to play in a World Series (with the 1932 Yankees) and play golf so well he played in the Masters Golf Tournament.

CHAPTER FIVE
NOTHING BUT
HALL OF FAMERS

1. Double: Which player holds the record for having played in the most big-league games without ever being ejected from one? At one time he also held the NL record for the most lifetime base hits.

2. Single: Only one man has ever appeared in 25 All-Star Games, and that is fitting because he is arguably one of the top three players of all time. Even though he last played a big-league game in 1976, he's still the all-time leader for such key statistics as runs driven in, extra-base hits, and total bases. He played for 23 seasons and averaged almost precisely 100 RBIs over that period of time, finishing with a gaudy 2,297 runs driven in. Name this 1982 inductee into the Hall of Fame.

3. Double: Which two men bashed more home runs while teammates than any other teammate combo?

4. Double: The first pitcher to eclipse Walter Johnson's lifetime strikeout total was Nolan Ryan, but before he firmly and finally grabbed hold of the record for good, another pitcher passed Ryan. For some time they took turns in the no. 1 slot on the list. Who was the man who battled Ryan for the top spot? Clue: he was once traded for Rick Wise in one of the worst trades ever engineered by the St. Louis Cardinals.

5. Double: He played third base. His real first name was Harold. What was his food-related nickname?

6. Home Run: From the department of Ancient Baseball History—a player who lasted from 1888 through 1903 was one of *five* brothers who made it to the majors. His personal problems with alcohol ultimately led to his death. In 1903, he became drunk, unruly, and combative on a train ride, causing the conductor to force him off the train. Ultimately, the player walked onto a bridge over the Niagara River then either jumped or stumbled, plunging into the river. His body was later recovered by the bottom of the Horseshoe Falls, dead at the age of 35. Name this lifetime .346 hitter.

7. Triple: This man was honored in an unusual way— he had his uniform number retired while he was still active. The White Sox retired his jersey number not long after they traded him to Texas. He was just 30 years old. He didn't retire until he was 42 and back in the White Sox uniform.

8. Home Run: Name the two legends, both outfielders, who wound up as Philadelphia Athletics in 1928 due mainly to strong indications that they had bet on baseball games (and some sources say they conspired to fix a game when they were with the teams they were most associated with).

9. Single: How many players who spent their entire career as a Yankee compiled 3,000+ hits?

10. Double: In all, 10 men in the 3,000-hit club managed to amass all of their hits with just one club—name six of them. Bonus: take credit for a home run if you can name eight or more of these men.

11. Double: Only one Hall of Fame pitcher was victimized for the 3,000th hit of a big-leaguer. Name this man who began as a skilled starter then became a great reliever.

12. Double: Although a fine offensive player, from 2000 through 2020 only one catcher allowed 125 stolen bases (in 2012). That man also led the NL in that dubious category five years in a row, and 10 seasons in all.

13. Single: What Houston great led his league in steals surrendered by a catcher from 1989 through 1991? In 1991, he made the All-Star squad for the first time.

14. Home Run: In his second full season, 1922, this Indians infielder struck out 20 times. In 1925, he struck out four times and that's over 699 plate appearances! From 1925 through his final season of 1933, he averaged 5 1/3 strikeouts per season. He could hit the ball, too. He had 436 doubles and a .312 lifetime batting average, meaning he was certainly not an easy out. Identify this great contact hitter.

15. Single: Baseball knowledge and/or common sense

should solve this one—who was the first player to top 400 total bases in a season?

16. Double: One year after the 400 TB plateau was reached, this man became the first NL player to attain that level.

17. Single: Since 1881, when Cap Anson set the record for career total bases, four men have surpassed his mark. Name two of them. Identify three or all four and you've stretched your hit into a double.

18. Single: Babe Ruth was the first player to compile 100+ extra-base hits in a season. Which Yankee was the first man ever to enjoy two seasons with 100 or more extra-base hits?

19. Home Run: Who was the first NL player to put up two seasons with 100 or more extra-base hits? Clue: he was an MVP once and he mainly starred with the Phillies.

20. Double: From 1933 until 1948, no NL player reached the 100 extra-base hits level. Who snapped that dry spell?

21. Single: How many times did Hank Aaron strike out 100 or more times in a season?

22. Double: How many combined times did team-mates Babe Ruth and Lou Gehrig reach 100+ strikeouts in a given season?

23. Single: How many times did Ruth lead his league in times striking out? a. 5 b. 0 c. 10

24. Double: When Hank Aaron joined the 3,000-hit club in 1970, he was the first man to reach that level since what other NL legend achieved this feat in 1958?

25. Single: Stan Musial held the record for the most hits in NL play for a long time. Who eventually eclipsed his record?

26. Single: Shockingly, in 2012 a Hall of Famer's mother was kidnapped. Fortunately, she was returned to the street she lived on about a day after being whisked away, taken from her vehicle.

27. Single: Rogers Hornsby is sometimes labeled the greatest right-handed hitter ever. He hit higher than .400 in three different seasons, tied for a record, and, as mentioned earlier, he hit .358 lifetime. True or false—despite all of that, he is not a member of the 3,000-hit club.

28. Double: Other than Hornsby, who is the only other man to hit .400 on three occasions during the modern era?

29. Single: True or false—Hornsby is the only player ever to smash 40 or more homers during a season in which he hit .400.

30. Double: Amazingly, in 1922 three players hit

higher than .400—Cobb, Hornsby, and what other player? Clues: this first baseman played for the St. Louis Browns and had a son who hit an historic home run in 1950. Name the third .400 hitter from 1922.

31. Double: Every trivia lover knows that Ted Williams is the last man to hit .400, but who was the last NL player to do this, hitting .401 in 1930 as the New York Giants first baseman?

32. Single: Who holds the NL record for hitting the most home runs in a Triple Crown–winning season? a. Hack Wilson b. Rogers Hornsby c. Stan Musial d. Willie Mays

33. Triple: Who has the overall record for the most home runs in a season during which he won the Triple Crown?

34. Single: Only one AL player has ever won the Triple Crown twice—name him.

35. Triple: Aside from Hornsby, what other St. Louis Cardinal won a Triple Crown?

36. Single: What Yankees slugger drove in the most runs ever in a Triple Crown season?

37. Home Run: Two Philadelphia players—one was with the Phillies, the other was with the Athletics—won Triple Crowns in the same season, 1933. Name both men.

38. Double: Which of the following players hit for the highest batting average (.426) in his Triple Crown season by an American League player? a. Willie Keeler b. Rogers Hornsby c. Nap Lajoie d. Ty Cobb

39. Double: Some trivia buffs like to expand the rare Triple Crown to an even more rare Quadruple Crown by requiring a Triple Crown winner to also lead his league in hits. Only two men have ever achieved that. Clues: one man did this in 1909, back when his nine homers led the AL, but there was nothing cheap about his 216 hits or his .377 batting average. The other player chalked up his Quadruple Crown nearly 60 years later.

40. Single: Six of the 13 players who put up a Triple Crown season did not win multiple MVP Awards. Name one.

41. Triple: Two of those six men from above never even won his league's MVP once. Name either player.

42. Single: What player had the lowest batting average ever for a Triple Crown winner? Clue: he won his Triple Crown with an AL team in the very first season after a NL team cast him off.

43. Double: Last question relating to the Triple Crown—three of the men to achieve that feat were in the midst of a hot streak during which they won back-to-back MVP trophies. That is to say, they won their Triple Crown in the year they won their first or their second of two MVPs in a row. Name one of the three all-time greats.

44. Triple: Through 2020, what pitcher had the highest single-season WAR ever?

45. Single: Through 2020, what position player had the best WAR in a season?

46. Single: What player, regardless of position played, owns the highest career WAR?

47. Double: What position player has the highest WAR in a season by a right-handed hitter as well as the best WAR by a NL player?

48. Double: Among the top men mentioned in Baseball Reference's list of single-season leaders and records for WAR for pitchers, this man had the best WAR among the pitchers who had their finest season based upon WAR after 1913. The man in question's top season came in the 1980s. Only two pitchers after the 1920s crack the top eight hurlers based on their finest single-season WAR rating (through the 2020 season). The first one has the third best WAR among pitchers, twice trailing only one man—the one who is the answer to question 44 above. Name the man referred to here, the one whose highest WAR came in the 1980s.

49. Double: The other post-1913 pitcher alluded to in the previous question had his finest season in the early

1970s. Name this man who is the highest ranked lefty on the WAR list in question.

50. Single: Can you identify this outstanding hitter? Due to being in the military during World War II, he played in just six seasons from 1941 through 1949. Despite that, he still was dominant, leading the AL in batting and home runs four times and in runs driven in three times. The year he returned from military service, 1946, he didn't skip a beat. Showing no signs of rust, he won the MVP Award, and the next season he was a Triple Crown winner.

51. Single: Name any of the top five hitters of all time based on the highest lifetime batting averages.

52. Single: Can you name any of the other men in the top 10 for highest lifetime batting average?

Players' ability to move from one club to another became much easier once the era of free agency came along. While many old-time greats played for just one team (or just a few) over their careers, that's not the case very often of late. Here are several questions relating to those two trends.

53. Single: First, list two of the four teams Vladimir Guerrero played for to earn a single. If you can name three of those teams, take a triple, and all four of them earns you a home run.

54. Single: Joe Morgan was a major leaguer for 22 years, spending time with five clubs. Your job is to identify three of them, but if you can name four or five, take a double.

55. Home Run: Steve Carlton is most famous for his great seasons with the Phillies, but he was with five other teams (three of them for just one year). You must name four of them.

56. Double: Even some great players from the days prior to free agency played for several teams. Sometimes, as was the case with Warren Spahn, a star latched on to one or more teams after his glory days with his original club in order to cling to his career. Name all three teams Spahn pitched for.

57. Single: Arguably, the two men who remain the greatest home run hitters of all time had something else in common. Both men started their career in one big-league city, gained the majority of their fame with one franchise, then returned to their "original" city—but with a *different team* and in a different league than they first signed with—at the very tail end of their playing days. Name these men.

58. Single: Now, there have been quite a few greats who were only with one team for their entire career. Again, since the days of free agency, this has become a bit more rare, but the next few questions pertain to one-team players. Start with an easy one—name the San Diego Padre who hit a personal high of .394 in 1994.

59. Single: Name both of the one-team players from

these clues—one hit a personal high of .390 in 1980 and is a member of the 3,000-hit club; the other player, who also had 3,000+ hits, is the ultimate Iron Man of baseball.

60. Single: Which of these men did not play his entire career with just one team? a. Ernie Banks b. Johnny Bench c. Craig Biggio d. Rod Carew

61. Single: Which of these men did not play his entire career with just one team? a. Jeff Bagwell b. Lou Brock c. Whitey Ford d. Chipper Jones

62. Double: Who was the oldest AL player ever to win a batting crown?

63. Triple: Name the player who holds the record for the longest gaps between his first batting crown and his final one. He spent his entire career in the AL.

64. Triple: Name the NL luminary who is tied for the second longest span between winning his first and his last batting title, which is also the all-time NL record.

65. Double: What was the first major-league club that Randy Johnson pitched for, making his debut in 1988?

66. Home Run: What team owned Christy Mathewson, but traded him to the New York Giants for pitcher Amos Rusie before the 1900 season began? Mathewson, therefore, made his big-league debut with the Giants, and the club in question would rue the trade forever. It was one of the worst trades in baseball history because Mathewson lasted 17 seasons and won 373 games in all. Rusie, on the other hand, achieved virtually nothing for his new club. He pitched in three contests, went 0–1, and put up an ERA of 8.59.

67. Double: What was the first big-league club that Orlando Cepeda was with? He was the 1958 NL Rookie of the Year after leading the league in doubles with 38.

68. Home Run: What team was the last of the eight clubs Gaylord Perry pitched for?

69. Triple: Where did Chicago Cubs great Billy Williams finish his big-league days? Clue: it was a team in the AL West.

70. Home Run: Which AL team was Bert Blyleven with when he hung up his cleats for good?

71. Single: Which pitcher began his career with the Dodgers in 1992, working on the same staff as his brother Ramon, before moving on to throw for the Expos, Red Sox, Mets, and finally, in 2009, for the Phillies?

72. Single: Which catcher wore no. 27 at the beginning of his career with Boston, but flipped those two digits around to no. 72 when he went from being a Red Sox to a White Sox player?

73. Single: In 1969, the top two position players in the

NL MVP voting both wore no. 44. Together, they would pile up 1,276 home runs. Name them.

74. Single: Name the infielder who abruptly and unexpectedly announced his retirement after playing 57 games in 1994. Hitting just .238, he said he had lost "the edge that it takes to play . . ." so he quit, walking away from about $15 million left on his contract. Two years later, at the age of 36, he returned to the game and showed he still had some high octane left in his tank, hitting 25 homers and driving home 92 runs.

75. Single: When Mariano Rivera, all-time leader for saves with 652, entered games, he figuratively put opponents' bats to sleep, and dispatched the players to bed. That ability earned him a nickname. What was it?

76. Single: Donora, Pennsylvania, never had a population of more than around 15,000, yet this town produced an All-Star Game MVP who was a starting player for the Big Red Machine, Ken Griffey Sr. Not only that, this was also the birthplace of two Hall of Famers, Stan Musial and Ken Griffey Jr. What nicknames that relate to stages of life did those Hall of Famers have?

77. Double: Sometimes a player's nickname is used for him almost constantly, so that his real name might get lost in the shuffle. What was the first name of Catfish Hunter?

78. Double: Who is the oldest pitcher ever to throw a perfect game, doing this in 2004?

79. Single: What man outdid the pitcher from the last question *in one respect*—age—when he became the oldest pitcher to throw a no-hitter? He was an astonishing 44 years and 90 days old when he no-hit the Toronto Blue Jays in 1991, the last of his multiple no-hitters.

80. Single: The pitcher from the previous question threw three more no-hitters than the next man on the no-hit list. Who ranks second? a. Bob Feller b. Sandy Koufax c. Randy Johnson

81. Double: Name the pitcher who once was the second oldest man to fire a no-hitter. What made him so incredible was the fact that although he spent 21 seasons in the majors, his first no-hitter didn't take place until his 16th season when he was 39. Then, the very next season, the 40-year-old lefty threw another no-hitter.

82. Single: For those purists who don't like to give credit to players whose names were tainted by playing during the Steroid Age and putting up suspicious stats, what great first baseman held the record for many decades for the most career grand slams with 23?

83. Single: Who holds the record for having pitched the most games in which he struck out 10 or more batters?

84. Double: Who ranks second behind the pitcher in the previous question?

85. Triple: What pitcher holds the record for having

the most wins in a season in which he did not win the Cy Young Award? This took place in 1968.

86. Single: Who did win the 1968 Cy Young Award?

87. Single: Name three of the first five men to amass 500 or more doubles and 500+ homers.

The year 2020 was a horrible one that was marred all over the world by COVID-19. It was also a year that shocked the baseball world because so many greats of the game passed away. Sadly, team tailors were kept busy sewing a slew of commemorative patches on jerseys to mourn those who passed on. Seven Hall of Famer players died in 2020. Furthermore, extending from August of 2020 and into 2021, nine Hall of Famers (counting manager Tommy Lasorda) died over a period of less than five months.

The answers to the questions 88 through 96 are all from the list of those who died from 2020 and, barely, into 2021.

88. Single: Who was the first player to compile 600+ doubles and 600 or more home runs?

89. Double: Baseball expert Bill James ranked this man as the greatest second baseman of all time.

90. Single: This man barely missed out on having a career .300 batting average at .297, and nearly joined the 400 HR club, falling one home run shy of that plateau. However, he was an 18-time All-Star who won 10 Gold Gloves while patrolling right field. He accomplished all of that having never even played a day in the minors. Name him.

91. Single: This outfielder led the NL in steals eight times, accomplishing that over a nine-year stretch from 1966 through 1974.

92. Single: Who recorded an unbelievable ERA of 1.12 one year during the 1960s, giving him the third lowest single-season ERA ever, and, by far, the lowest ERA by a pitcher after 1920?

93. Double: What winner of 324 games only won 20 or more games once, but over his career which ran from 1966 through 1988, he led the NL in WHIP four times (three times with the Dodgers and once with the Astros)? Durable, he was also the first pitcher to strike out 100 or more batters in 20 consecutive seasons.

94. Single: What starting pitcher, through 2020, had the highest percentage of votes when he was inducted into the Hall of Fame?

95. Single: Which pitcher began his career as a reliever for the Milwaukee Braves before becoming a starter who won 318 games over a long, 24-year career?

96. Single: Name the man who attended high school in New York City then wound up playing his entire 16-year career with the Yankees where he won 236 games. Clue: he was the 1961 Cy Young Award winner after going 25–4.

97. Double: Who set a record by winning the home-run crown seven seasons in a row?

98. Double: Babe Ruth owns the most home-run titles with 12 (once with only 11 HRs), but who is second on the all-time list with eight, which is also the most ever in NL play?

99. Single: Who holds the record for the most career runs driven in with 2,297, a record he's held since since 1975 when he passed Ruth's RBI total?

100. Single: What 6'6" outfielder was drafted not only by a major-league team in the first round (1973), but also by an NFL team and two pro basketball teams from the NBA and old ABA?

101. Double: Which southpaw pitcher was drafted in the second round by a big-league club in June of 1984, and in the fourth round by the Los Angeles Kings of the NHL that same month?

102. Double: What terrific pitcher, a former Rookie of the Year who plied his trade from 1967 through 1986, set the record for the most consecutive strikeouts in a game?

103. Single: Which member of the 500-home-run club is the only man to play for the Braves when they were located in Boston, Milwaukee, and Atlanta?

104. Double: Albert Pujols and another great power

hitter share the NL record for the most grand slams in a season. Name that player.

105. Double: For this, the 512th and final question, name the two Hall of Famers who are tied on the all-time home-run list with 512 HRs.

CHAPTER FIVE ANSWERS: NOTHING BUT HALL OF FAMERS

1. Stan Musial. The genial St. Louis Cardinals outfielder/first baseman played in more than 3,000 games (3,026 to be exact) and never once was given the thumb by an umpire. Next best on the list is Willie Mays (2,992) followed by yet three more Hall of Famers: Brooks Robinson (2,896), Robin Yount (2,856), and, according to one source, Tony Perez (2,777)—he was kicked out of one game, but that was when he was managing. Interestingly, all 13 of the men atop this list are Hall of Famers.

Here's a vivid example of why Musial never got the thumb. On April 18, 1954, Musial laced an RBI double, and due to poor defensive plays, Musial also scored on a Little League–like "home run." However, an umpire ruled that the hit was foul and wiped out the play. Two Cardinals got ejected for arguing vociferously, but Musial calmly spoke with the ump. Satisfied with an explanation, he genially philosophized, "Well, there's nothing you can do about it." But there was something Musial could do about it—he connected again, banging out a legitimate double.

Veteran umpire Tom Gorman once stated, "The bigger the guy, the less he argues. You never heard a word out of Stan Musial." Only once, in a Class D game, did Musial, then only 19, get the thumb.

2. Hank Aaron. Many fans and experts feel Hammerin' Hank is still the legitimate all-time home-run king. If that was the case, he would have held the career homer record for an eternity, since 1974.

For any player to hold such a venerable record for so long a period of time is almost impossible to fathom. By way of comparison, Babe Ruth hit his 714th homer in 1935, and that total stood as the apex until 1974. Another example: experts all agreed that nobody would top Lou Gehrig's lifetime iron-man record of having played in 2,130 consecutive games, which was set early in the 1939 season. However, even that astonishing mark didn't endure. Cal Ripken Jr. shattered it in 1995. Final example—Nolan Ryan has been the all-time King of K's since he retired in 1993. Actually, he took over the top slot even before that, then added to his record until he hung up the cleats at the brittle age of 46.

3. Hank Aaron and Eddie Mathews. They were members of the Braves franchise, playing together from 1954 through 1966. They combined for 863 homers to eclipse the old record of 859 home runs slugged by Yankees legends Lou Gehrig and Babe Ruth. The third highest total by teammates belongs to Willie Mays and Willie McCovey, who struck the 801 HRs as Giants.

4. Steve Carlton. After being traded, "Lefty" went on to win 241 over 15 seasons with the Phillies; Wise won 32 for St. Louis over two years.

5. Pie Traynor

6. Ed Delahanty

7. Harold Baines

8. Tris Speaker and Ty Cobb. Originally they were to be forced into retirement until Commissioner Kenesaw Mountain Landis intervened.

9. One, Derek Jeter

10. Jeter, Carl Yastrzemski, Robin Yount, Stan Musial, Cal Ripken Jr., George Brett, Tony Gwynn, Craig Biggio, Al Kaline, and Roberto Clemente

11. Dennis Eckersley gave up Dave Winfield's 3,000th hit.

12. Mike Piazza

13. Craig Biggio—of course he was later shifted to second base and the outfield. In his worst season, he gave up 140 stolen bases, but that's a far cry from the obscure, ancient mark of 205.

14. Joe Sewell. Over 14 seasons he whiffed 114 times. A modern slugger can reach that total in about half a season.

15. Babe Ruth (1921) with 457, still a record

16. Rogers Hornsby with 450 in 1922

17. Honus Wagner broke Anson's record first, followed by Ty Cobb, Stan Musial, and Hank Aaron.

18. Lou Gehrig in 1927 and 1930. Ruth had 119 in 1921, still no. 1.

19. Chuck Klein in 1930 and 1932

20. Stan Musial with 103

21. b. Zero

22. Zero

23. a. five times, with a high point of 93

24. Stan Musial

25. Pete Rose, on his way to owning the MLB record

26. Cal Ripken Jr. Previously a pitcher named Ugueth Urbina suffered the same fate. His mother was rescued, unharmed, but after a grueling five months.

27. True. Hornsby wound up with 2,930 hits. Another Hornsby feat: he not only won two Triple Crowns, but his cumulative stats for the decade of the 1920s gave him a triple crown of that 10-year period, a very rare achievement.

28. Ty Cobb. He hit .400 in back-to-back seasons (1911 and 1912) then again many years later in 1922. Ed Delahanty went over the .400 mark three times, but did so before the turn of the century in 1894, 1895, and 1899.

29. True

30. George Sisler. His son Dick only hit .276 lifetime to his father's .340, but on the final day of the 1950 season Dick hit a 10th-inning home run to snap a 1–1 tie with the Brooklyn Dodgers, eliminating them from the pennant race and giving the Phillies their first flag since 1915.

Actually, now that MLB has recognized Negro League players as true major leaguers, there was a fourth man to top .400 in 1922, Heavy Johnson, who hit .406. He hit exactly .406 again the next season on his way to winning a Triple Crown with the Kansas City Monarchs.

31. Bill Terry

32. b. Again, the answer is Rogers Hornsby. His 42 HRs in 1922, when he hit .401, is the most ever for a NL Triple Crown winner. By the way, none of the other men listed in this multiple-choice question ever won a Triple Crown.

33. Mickey Mantle. He swatted 52 home runs when he won his Triple Crown in 1956.

34. Ted Williams. In his first Triple Crown season, 1942, he didn't awe MVP voters as he came in 21 votes behind AL MVP Joe Gordon of the Yankees. Voters overlooked the edge Williams had over Gordon in WAR, 10.5 to 7.7, in favor of Gordon's contribution to his pennant-winning team. When Williams won his second Triple Crown in 1947, he was once more denied an MVP trophy. That went to Yankees star Joe DiMaggio, whose team became World Champions that year. Williams was with a third-place Boston team. Still, his WAR that season was more than double that of DiMaggio, 9.6 to 4.7!

35. Joe Medwick in 1937. His 31 home runs tied with Mel Ott for the NL lead. Medwick is also the last NL player to accomplish this feat. If you throw in a pre-1900 St. Louis player from the old American Association, the Cards franchise produced four Triple Crown winners, most ever.

36. Lou Gehrig. He racked up 166 RBIs in 1934 when he also tied his personal high for homers with 49 and hit a lusty .363. Unbelievably, that season he finished behind a Yankees teammate in the MVP voting *and*, in all there were four players who finished higher than Gehrig in the MVP balloting. The award went to Mickey

Cochrane of the pennant-winning Detroit Tigers who earned 67 points in the voting to Gehrig's 54. The Yankee who pulled in more MVP votes than Gehrig was pitcher Lefty Gomez who won 26 games and had an ERA of 2.33. The other players who were ahead of the Iron Horse were also on the Tigers: Charlie Gehringer with a .356 batting average, 11 HRs, and 127 RBIs; and Schoolboy Rowe, who went 24–8.

37. Chuck Klein and Jimmie Foxx. Despite his Triple Crown, Klein, who had won the MVP Award the year before, only finished second in the 1933 voting, way behind Giants pitcher Carl Hubbell (77 points to 48). The Giants won the pennant while the Phillies, losers of 92 games, finished next to last in the standings. In the meantime, Foxx won the AL MVP in both 1932 and in his '33 Triple Crown season.

38. c. Lajoie. In fact, his .426 batting average in 1901 has stood the test of a long time, still standing as the highest batting average in his Triple Crown season by an American League player.

39. The two men were Ty Cobb and Carl Yastrzemski. For Yaz, his 44 homers, 121 ribbies represented personal highs. His career batting average of .285 was 41 points lower than what he hit in his Triple Crown season of 1967.

40. Carl Yastrzemski, Joe Medwick, Chuck Klein, Ty Cobb, Nap Lajoie, and Heinie Zimmerman. It should be noted that the RBI was not an official stat until 1920, so some sources don't count the Triple Crowns of players such as Cobb, Lajoie, and Zimmerman.

41. Lajoie and Zimmerman

42. Frank Robinson, who hit .316 when he won the Triple Crown. He spent 1965 with Reds when he was 30 years old for almost the entire season. From his rookie season of 1956 through '65, he finished in the top 20 in MVP voting every year but one, and he was usually in the top 10. He was even the fourth highest vote-getter in the MVP balloting of 1964. However, after the '65 season, the Reds' front office were convinced he was too old, so they swapped him to the Baltimore Orioles for a 29-year-old pitcher who went 1–5 in his two years with the Reds; a 22-year-old outfielder who lasted just 136 games in a Cincinnati uniform; and Milt Pappas who, in three seasons with the Reds, went 30–29. Meanwhile, Robinson not only led Baltimore to a World Championship in his first season with the O's, he also put up these numbers to win his Triple Crown: he slammed 49 home runs and drove home 122 runs to go with his previously mentioned .316 batting average. He topped it off by taking home his MVP Award that season, becoming the first (and through 2020, the only) player to win the award in both leagues.

43. Jimmie Foxx won his Triple Crown in 1933, the second year of his back-to-back MVP seasons. Mickey Mantle was next with his "crown" in 1956, the first season of his consecutive MVP years. Finally, Miguel

Cabrera's first of two successive MVP seasons was 2012, the year he turned in a Triple Crown season.

44. Walter Johnson in 1913. That year he had a WAR of 15.1 based on his 36 victories, his 1.14 ERA, and his .837 winning percentage. Johnson also owns the second highest single-season WAR among modern-era pitchers (13.2 in 1912).

45. Babe Ruth in 1923 with a WAR of 14.2. A few of his key statistics from that season include his 151 runs scored, 41 HRs, 130 RBIs, and his 1.309 on-base plus slugging percentage. For those who don't fully buy into WAR as an end-all stat, compare Ruth's stats in a few other seasons. For example, in 1921, he scored 177 times, amassed 59 homers, drove in a whopping 168 runs in 152 contests, and had a slightly higher on-base plus slugging percentage than he did in '23 at 1.359. Yet his WAR for 1921 was lower, at 12.9, than it was in 1923. WAR is a complex stat, so you be the judge.

46. Ruth at a staggering 183.1, which is 18.3 points better than the second man on the lifetime WAR list, Walter Johnson.

47. Rogers Hornsby at 12.3 in 1924

48. Dwight Gooden had a WAR of 12.2 in 1985.

49. Steve Carlton was at 12.1 in 1972.

50. Ted Williams. From 1941 through 1949, he won both of his MVP Awards, came in second three times, and finished in third place the other season.

51. Ty Cobb ranks first at .3662 (for many years sources had his batting average at .367). He's followed by Oscar Charleston at .3643, Rogers Hornsby at .3585, then Shoeless Joe Jackson (.3558) and Jud Wilson (.3519).

52. Lefty O'Doul's .3493 places him no. 6 all-time. Next is Turkey Stearnes, who hit .3490. Ignoring Ed Delahanty (.3458) because the bulk of his career was spent prior to our modern era, Tris Speaker checks in at no. 8 (.3447). Billy Hamilton and his .3444 also gets passed up for the same reason as Delahanty, so the no. 9 slot belongs to Ted Williams ,who also hit .3444. After skipping Dan Brouthers (.3424), Babe Ruth rounds out the top 10 at .3421.

53. Guerrero began his major-league days with the Expos for eight seasons. He was an Angel for six more years. The tough part of this question pertains to the fact that he was with his final two clubs, the Rangers and Orioles, for just one season each.

54. Morgan began his career with the Houston Colt.45s in 1963 before moving on to the Cincinnati Reds. Then, after one year back in Houston, came a sometimes forgotten two-year stay with the Giants, and one season with the Phillies before he retired after one final season spent with Oakland.

55. Carlton played for these teams in addition to the Phillies: the Cardinals, Twins, Giants, Indians, and White Sox.

56. Of Spahn's 21 seasons in the majors, all but one featured him in a Braves uniform. In 1965, his last season, he still managed to start 30 games and work close to 200 innings at the age of 44. He split that final season between the Mets and the Giants.

57. Hank Aaron broke into the majors as a NL player in Milwaukee with the Braves and spent 21 years as a Brave. After a trade, he spent his final two seasons back in Milwaukee, but this time as a Brewer in the AL. Meanwhile, Babe Ruth started out in Boston with the Red Sox (and was there for six years), but he achieved most of his fantastic feats as a Yankee. Then, he played one year in the NL as a member of the Boston Braves.

58. Tony Gwynn. He won a batting crown in his first full season, added three in a row (1987 through 1989), then four more consecutive titles from 1994 through 1997. He had many opportunities to leave San Diego for more illustrious franchises, but he stayed put.

59. George Brett and Cal Ripken Jr.

60. d. Rod Carew. He was with the Twins and Angels.

61. b. Lou Brock. He began with the Cubs then became a Cardinal.

62. Ted Williams. When he won his last batting title of six, he was 40 years and 29 days old. He did this in 1958 when he hit .328.

63. Ted Williams. His first batting title came in 1941, the year he hit .406, and, as mentioned above, his last crown came in 1958 for a gap of 17 years.

64. Stan Musial. In his case, he copped a batting title for the first time in 1943 and his last one came along in 1957, for a 14-year gap. In the AL, George Brett also went 14 years between winning his first crown in 1976 and his final one in 1990.

65. Johnson began his big-league days with the Montreal Expos.

66. Mathewson was first purchased by the Giants from the minors, but went to the Cincinnati Reds in a Rule 5 draft. It was the Reds, then, who wound up dealing him to the Giants. The Reds controlled two future Hall of Famers and got a grand total of one win out of them as the only thing they had to show for acquiring those talented pitchers. Rusie was a great pitcher, but way over the hill when Cincinnati obtained him. Mathewson was young and untested when with the Reds, but what a future he had. For the record, Mathewson's only victory with Cincinnati came in his final season after the Reds traded with the Giants—this time to obtain Mathewson.

67. The San Francisco Giants

68. Perry ended his 22 years in the majors with the Kansas City Royals in 1983. He began that season with the Mariners, but his final 14 mound appearances were with the Royals. He was even involved in George Brett's Pine Tar game. After the umpires declared Brett out for using an illegal bat, Perry, known to be involved in chicanery of another sort, seized the bat and tried to run away with the evidence, but he was caught in the act and was ejected from the wild game.

69. Williams wrapped up his 18-year major-league stint with Oakland.

70. Blyleven threw his last pitch for the California Angels.

71. Pedro Martinez

72. Carlton Fisk. His jersey numbers were retired by both Boston and Chicago.

73. MVP Willie McCovey (521 career home runs) and third-place vote-getter, Hank Aaron (755 lifetime homers). Tom Seaver came in second in the voting.

74. Ryne Sandberg

75. The Sandman. Beginning in 1999, when he entered games his personal theme song, *Enter Sandman*, was played over Yankee Stadium's P.A. system.

76. In Musial, you've got The Man. With Junior, you've got The Kid.

77. James (Augustus) Hunter went by Jim when not identified as Catfish.

78. Randy Johnson. He was 40 years old (plus seven months) when he crafted his perfect game for Arizona, mowing down 27 straight Braves. The previous record belonged to Cy Young, who was 37 years of age when he threw his perfecto in 1904.

79. Nolan Ryan's seventh no-hitter, a mind-boggling record of its own, made him the oldest no-hit artist ever.

80. Sandy Koufax. His four no-hitters came in consecutive seasons from 1962 through 1965.

81. Warren Spahn. At the time of Spahn's no-hitters, only Cy Young (in 1908) had ever thrown a no-hitter at an older age than Spahn.

82. Lou Gehrig. Alex Rodriguez ended his days with 25 grand slams.

83. Nolan Ryan. He fanned 10 or more men 215 times.

84. Randy Johnson. He struck out 10+ batters 212 times—nobody else is close to Ryan and Johnson.

85. Juan Marichal. In 1968, he went 26–9 and came up empty in the voting for the Cy Young Award—literally getting zero votes for that honor. What's more incredible is the fact that the Dominican Dandy, who didn't even start more than 27 games until 1962, was among the top 10 in ERA seven seasons of the 1960s, and in the top five for wins six times—four of those times he ranked first or second in the NL for victories (hitting 25+ wins three times), yet he went through that *entire decade without ever earning a single vote* for the Cy Young Award. The only time he cracked the top 10 was in 1971 when he came in eighth in the voting with just one vote.

86. Bob Gibson was the reason Marichal didn't get a vote in 1968: Gibson was the unanimous Cy Young Award selection. He also was the NL MVP based on his 22–9 record with 13 shutouts to go with 268 K's.

87. Babe Ruth, Ted Williams, Hank Aaron, Willie Mays, and Frank Robinson

88. Aaron, who passed away in January of 2021. He wound up with 624 doubles and 755 HRs.

89. Joe Morgan. Bill James ranked Morgan ahead of Eddie Collins and Rogers Hornsby.

90. Al Kaline. He broke in with his Tigers as an 18-year-old, directly out of high school.

91. Lou Brock. He is in the 3,000-hit club, but, unlike many fellow members, at .293 he didn't own a lifetime batting average of .300 or better.

92. Bob Gibson. He finished in the top five for the best ERA seven times, but 1968 was the only season in which he led the league in that department.

93. Don Sutton

94. Tom Seaver. He pulled down 98.84 percent of the votes cast when he was voted into the Hall of Fame, omitted on five of the 430 votes cast in 1992. Among pitchers, only reliever Mariano Rivera, inducted unanimously, did better.

95. Phil Niekro. His 300th win came via a shutout, making him the oldest pitcher to ever throw a shutout. Impressive given that among all 300-game winners, this man owned the fewest victories by the time he turned 30, just 31.

96. Whitey Ford. Several other big-name players, albeit not Hall of Famers, died in 2020. That list includes Dick Allen, Johnny Antonelli, Glenn Beckert, Tony Fernandez, Jay Johnstone, Don Larsen, Mike McCormick, Lindy McDaniel, Bob Watson, and Jimmy Wynn.

97. Ralph Kiner. He led or tied for the NL lead in homers from 1946 through 1952. He did have low totals in the first and last year of that streak, 23 and 37, and he did share the league lead with Johnny Mize twice (1947 and 1948), and once with Hank Sauer (1952), but he also belted 47, 51, and 54 homers in his three best seasons. Also, it's noteworthy that the seven years he dominated the power category were his first seven seasons in the majors.

98. Mike Schmidt

99. Hank Aaron. His 2,297 RBIs over 23 seasons means he averaged almost precisely 100 runs driven in each year, a fantastic mark of consistent greatness. In fact, when based on an average of how many RBIs he had per 162 games played, he averaged 113 ribbies each "season."

100. Dave Winfield. He even excelled as a college pitcher (9–1, 2.74 ERA as a senior, and 19–4, 2.24 overall with 229 strikeouts over 169 innings) before jumping straight to the majors. The Minnesota Vikings drafted him in the 17th round, knowing of his athleticism and ignoring the fact that he had never played football in high school or in college. One source says he is one of only three men to be drafted by pro baseball, basketball, and football teams.

101. Tom Glavine. He was drafted by the Kings ahead of future Hall of Famers Luc Robitaille and Brett Hull.

102. Tom Seaver. His record was tied by both Corbin Burnes and Aaron Nola in 2021.

103. Eddie Mathews. He played in Boston during the Braves' final season there (1952), in Milwaukee from 1953 through 1965, and in Atlanta during their first season there, 1966.

104. Ernie Banks, with five in 1955. Pujols matched him in 2009.

105. Eddie Mathews and Ernie Banks

SOURCES USED

BOOKS:
1960: When the Pittsburgh Pirates Had Them All the Way by
  Wayne Stewart
Baseballistics Edited by Bert Randolph Sugar
Baseball's Book of Firsts by Lloyd Johnson
Mike Hargrove and the Cleveland Indians by Jason Ingraham
The New Biographical History of Baseball by Donald Dewey
  and Nicholas Acocella
Over the Edge by Jay Johnstone and Rick Talley
A Picture Postcard History of Baseball by Ron Menchine
Sweet '60: The 1960 Pirates by Clifton Blue Parker

MAGAZINES:
Baseball Digest (various issues)

WEBSITES:
Baseball Almanac
Baseball Reference
http://exhibits.baseballhalloffame.org/dressed_to_the
  _nines/numbers.htm
https://www.si.com/mlb/2021/04/16/david-samson-barry
  -bonds-marlins-hitting-coach-disaster

OTHER BOOKS BY THE AUTHOR

1960: When the Pittsburgh Pirates Had Them All the Way
Alex Rodriguez: A Biography
All the Moves I Had
America's Football Factory
Babe Ruth: A Biography
Baseball Bafflers
Baseball Dads
Baseball Oddities
Baseball's Oddities
Baseball Puzzlers
Behind the Scenes with the Cleveland Indians
Fathers, Sons, and Baseball
The Gigantic Book of Baseball Quotations (Editor)
Great Tales of Baseball
Hitting Secrets of the Pros
Indians on the Game
The Little Giant Book of Basketball Facts
Match Wits with Baseball Experts
Name That Ballplayer
Pitching Secrets of the Pros
Remembering the Greatest Coaches and Games of the NFL Glory Years
Remembering the Stars of the NFL Glory Years
Stan the Man: The Life and Times of Stan Musial
Tales from First Base

ABOUT THE AUTHOR

Wayne Stewart was born in Pittsburgh and raised in Donora, Pennsylvania, a town that produced four big-league baseball players, including Stan Musial and the father-son Griffeys. Stewart was on the same Donora High School baseball team as classmate Griffey Sr.

Stewart began covering sports in 1978, freelancing for publications such as *Baseball Digest, Beckett Baseball Card Monthly, Baseball Bulletin, Boys' Life,* and for official team publications of 10 major-league clubs, including the Braves, Orioles, Boston Red Sox, Yankees, and Dodgers.

He has interviewed sports immortals such as Joe Montana, Mike Ditka, Don Maynard, Larry Bird, George Gervin, Robert Parish, Nolan Ryan, Bob Gibson, Rickey Henderson, and Ken Griffey Jr., and has written biographies of Babe Ruth, Stan Musial, and Alex Rodriguez. In addition, he has written books ranging from *Fathers, Sons, and Baseball* to *All the Moves I Had,* the autobiography he co-wrote with Hall of Fame wide receiver Raymond Berry.

This is his 36th book. Stewart has appeared as a baseball expert/historian on numerous radio and television shows including an ESPN Classic program, on ESPN radio, and on the Pat Williams radio program. He also hosted radio shows for a Lorain, Ohio, station including pre-game reports prior to Notre Dame football games and Cleveland Indians baseball games, and a call-in talk show. He has written for several newspapers, and some of his works have been used in eight anthologies.

A teacher for 31 years, Stewart now lives in Amherst, Ohio.